HOW TO REPAIR YOUR CREDIT IN 180 DAYS

HOW TO REPAIR YOUR CREDIT IN 180 DAYS

By Robert Boyd

Published by

MIDNIGHT EXPRESS BOOKS

HOW TO REPAIR YOUR CREDIT IN 180 DAYS

ISBN-13: 978-0692268049

ISBN-10: 0692268049

Published by
MIDNIGHT EXPRESS BOOKS
POBox 69
Berryville AR 72616
(870) 210-3772
MEBooks1@yahoo.com

HOW TO REPAIR YOUR CREDIT IN 180 DAYS

By Robert Boyd

Special Thanks

Black Enterprise Magazine, Entrepreneur Magazine, USA Today Newspaper. The Wall Street Journal, Bloomberg Magazine. Lexis Nexis, and West Law, and BNA Court Reporter.

Acknowledgements

First of all I would like to give an honor to God who is the head of my life and I will never turn my back on Jesus.

Thank you Midnight Express. It's been truly an honor for you to publish my book.

To my mother, Linda Tribble; words cannot express how I feel about you but if they had an award for mother of the year, then you would receive the award every year mom! I have always and will always love you. I could not imagine life without you; who else will believe in me.

To my step dad, Leonard Tribble. You taught me to be a man and to get paid in the process. Because of you dad, they can't fade me. Who else could take the motor out of my truck and slap another one in a week later. You deserve the best.

To my sister Francesca. I miss you. I miss us. Maybe one day we can reconnect.

To Nakia, stay killing em.

April, thanks for the glance, even though it didn't last long. You passed my whole summer. To Brandi Boyd, thanks for being a rider in my time of need.

To granny, the day you gave up drinking was a great moment in my life. Thank you granny for showing us as a family what we are really made of even though most of them can't live up to the part. To grandma one more year grandma and I'm out. I miss you and I'll see you when I get there. To Grandma Juanita, once pops died, I never saw another man in your house. You are the true essence of what a real woman is and what she stands for.

James "Duke" Franklin, Tez, Bobby, Big Dawg, Frankie, Gloria, Missy, thanks for helping me feel like family and having my back. Y'all know what it is. Auletta, Peewee, Antonio.

To Uncle Carl and Aunt Beverly, I hope this book shows you I'm following your lead. And yes uncle, you were right. I'm done with the game; I should never have played. But it is what it is. To Aunt Shirley, I hope you are proud of this book I wrote. And I'm done with the bad things of life. You didn't raise me that way. And I'm sorry I let you down. I know Grandma Christine missed you and all of us and I miss her. Who else could teach me the difference between spoiled milk and good milk? I need to choose the method when I choose my women. Lyndsey Phelps, thanks for everything and shouts out to the crew: Temisha, Raven, Shon, Suglenda, Mnia, and Raven, Kesley, Reneta, and Charity. I miss all of you as friends. We shared some great times and never crossed one another. Some of us had physical relationships and some of us were just friends but all and all. Y'all were there for me in the beginning and I appreciate that. Shouts Out Tren, E, what's up Baby Savage , thanks to Mr. Serv On for laying the tracks, KLC from beats by the pound, Young Buck of G-Unit for keeping it trill and Big V of the Nappy Roots for the tracks baby. Desmond Bell, Desmond Johnson, and Young'n (AJ Hearney and his lil' brother, what's up?) when I get home it's on. We legit now though baby. From the suburbs, to prison, to politics, LET'S GO!

Rickey Shirley, my heart fell when we sped off and looked back and you didn't get in the truck like I thought you did. They don't raise 'em like you cuz. I still shed tears at night. I love and will always visit your grave. You are never forgotten.

Real Talk. Kelton Stockton, who else could I trust with $20,000 in cash to take a trip to Atlanta and bring it back. There wasn't no female my dawg Kelton couldn't pull, real talk. Marcus Lamont (Chyl) Crenshaw, you held me down and you were one of the smartest dudes I ever met besides myself (lol). You started me in this game baby and I'm gonna finish it legit, on top, like we dreamed. Y'all three, no truer three, that's real.

To my aunties, cousins, uncles, and associates, what it do. Y'all know what it is. I'm still on they heels man. I can't be stopped especially with God behind me. I'm coming for a million dollars this time. Y'all thought that $100 g's I had was something.

Trayvon Martin, you stood your ground and we are proud of you. You gave me the ambition to write and type this book in 14 days. You are the true essence of a well raised and trained African American because we don't back down to NOBODY.

We gone lift you up, the black community is with your family with love, thank you man. To the father's of the world, take care of your kids. There is nothing worse than a sorry man. Free Duke, A.K.A. Balla D, Fed Up, Corey Furgeson, Big Dame, Sauce, Sky, Big Shitty, Juice, William Partee, Jr., Kenneth Red Williams, Tyrail Curry, and Uncle Rusell Sublett what's up baby. I got y'all when I get home, for real. I know what it's like. Nathaniel Haskins what it do. Free patty Boy Rozelli, Bay Bay and Henry Patterson, Gerald Duffy, C-Murder, and Rest in Peace to my cousin D.D. Paul (we love and miss your presence bro), Star Damron, Selena and Janice Howard, Chris Jewell, and Billy Rice (you showed me what real love was all about for someone who wasn't related to a man and you will, always be a grandfather in my mind, thank you Billy, I love you for that), thanks to Marquez and Billy Kirk who held me down in JL French. Rest in Peace to Troy Hatchett (I would have never had a 100 g's if it wasn't for you big cuz. You was the man that made me who I am in the streets. From street corner to Kingpin. We rolling with Christ now though Troy. I wish you were here to see us win in God's name. We still the life of the party though; pass the Moet and Ciroc. LoL! Yo special shouts out to those who held me down in the library, Vel, S, Miller, Henry, and Bun, who kept me with the paper and pens. Larry and Junior in Unicor, y'all held me down in the beginning. I am forever grateful. Salute!

They told me to keep it short so some of y'all I cannot name and some of y'all no longer roll. But shouts out to Rob Jr. my son, I do this because of you man, Daddy gone ball like a dawg baby. Kadeshia, get you a degree so you can be your own women and will never have to need a man. Remember the person that loves the least has the most control in a relationship. Clarissa Haskins, even though we go through what we go through I will always love you and I pray that one day you will learn to let people love you instead of denying the obvious. Be good girl. Shouts out to Shardavia Coker for being there in the beginning and shouts out to all the females who got at me on all the online love sites. Keep hollering at yo boy. I'll be there in 2015 and I'm single ladies what's up!!!!! Eric Stockton what it do boy, Joey, Jamie, J. Renfro, Wayne, Uncle Wayne, Merida Sublett, RIP. Shout outs to Caverna High class of 97, Louisville, KY, Yazoo City Library staff and Gaines family. Cousin Calvin, RIP (died in Lagrange prison riot) we miss you. Uncle Calvin what it do? Bobby, Leonard, and Leon Page and Neal Bethel for always watching over me.

Uncle Laddell, Aunt Rissie, Tracey, and Tawana, Aunt Jean. I'm baaack!!! Slick, Maurice, Tonzo, Pee Wee, Phil and King. Rev Duke and Ms. Duke thanks for the support.

Contents

CHAPTER 1: Understanding Your Credit

Did you know that according to the "USA Today" a family with a gross income of $80,000 per year is estimated to have $12,500 in actual savings outside of their 401K and IRA savings? [Note that up to 30 percent borrowed from your IRA account and returned within 60 days is not taxable and exempt from being penalized. Meaning it will not cost you additional fees as long as the monies are returned within the limitations period]. With the average costs of homes and mortgages interest rates on the rise due to the economic struggle. A new home may cost you an average of $100,000 per year depending on the location and not to mention the rising cost of crude oil making it just as costly to drive to work and we haven't even mentioned the rising cost of college tuition for your first born nor living expenses. Many Americans will need credit at some point in their lives. The average score for an American citizen is estimated between 540 and 680, with the highest score peaking at an astonishing 840 and a moderate score of 700 to 840 needed for a loan for a home valued at around $150,000. Many Americans will either pay high interest for the homes of their dreams due to their late payments on other purchases that lowered their credit rating or they will be forced to pay rent for the next 20 years. Imagine riding down Sunset Boulevard in Los Angeles or Peach Tree Street in Atlanta, Georgia and noticing a pair of $600 Louboutin Red Bottoms for Easter Sunday or riding down a strip downtown and noticing a new or used Camaro for $18,000 which would put savings at flat zero after the purchase. [That's if you even have $600 or $18,000 in your checking or savings]. It would not be a great idea to borrow from your Roth IRA nor your personal savings. No, that is why credit is important and not just credit. Good credit, [a 650 to an 840 credit score]. Need more examples of why a person needs good credit. Imagine riding down 1-65 and your Head gasket blows on your used luxury sedan that is no longer under warranty. Your average income is $30,000 per year and you constantly dip into your checking account so much, that you don't even have room for a savings account. The cost of the gasket is around three to four hundred dollars and that is not accounting for the maintenance work needed or the diagnosis test. It would be great to call the bank for a floating personal loan, where the bank will allow personal checks written to companies for purchasing for you for an agreed upon amount and interest rate without showing up into the bank for a meeting. It would also be nice to always have leverage for fixed rates instead of regular rates which are subject to change upon delinquencies on your account for late payments because when banks form mergers or acquisitions with other companies they are not entitled to honor interest rates of delinquent accounts{ XE "delinquent accounts" }. [Banks don't tell you this when you sign for the loan agreement and why would they.

2

After they let you slide, then sell your loan to another bank due to its delinquencies. The chances that you will default on the loan is above average and the bank repossesses your vehicle or home and sells it to the next person who comes along and then they still report the repossession to your credit agency which lowers your score and makes it hard for you to finance a Playstation® 4 let alone a car or a home without filing bankruptcy.] This is what happens when you are late on your car payment or your cell bill. Your account becomes delinquent and subject to be purchased by other credit agencies at higher interest rates.

Or remember that cell bill you never paid. And you thought you were beating the system because you didn't pay your apple iPhone® bill and switched carriers to sprint and sprint wanted a $150 dollar deposit and you think you're winning because your bill for the iPhone® was $400. WRONG! The carrier for the Apple iPhone® which is called a furnisher{ XE "furnisher" }, will transfer the debt to collectors who will report to the three credit reporting Bureaus which will hold this delinquent account over your head for the next seven years. Guess what happened? Your credit score was just lowered. Now the debt that you think you ran from has came home to haunt you and the bill is now turned over to a debt collection agency and now they will not stop calling your phone. They will do a number of techniques such as blocking calls or disguising themselves as someone else just to verify that you are the person from who they have purchased the debt and the

3

next thing you know. They're garnishing your checks for this alleged debt. Not only now are they taking your money but the inquiry they made into your credit report{ XE "credit report" } has lowered your score. With these types of inferences happening in your daily life, you're headed for economic disaster and now that dream home you hoped to purchase or those Louboutins you wanted so bad to put on your new credit card will be at an interest rate so high, you'll default on the loan or credit card before the monies are ever paid back in full. With a 680 to an 840 credit score you're almost guaranteed a fixed rate at no more than 5 percent. With a credit score of 540 you're looking at an interest rate as high as 22 percent on credit cards as well as loans from finance companies or the bank and that new Mustang you just secured a loan for at $13,000 is going to end up costing you around $20 - $25,000. So you're paying brand new Dodge Challenger prices for a used Dodge charger, not to mention you probably need a cosigner before any bank will finance you. When you can't find a cosigner and you want to fix your credit, you're faced with three options. Purchasing a vehicle at a buy here/pay here lot for a high interest rate, paying an attorney to file bankruptcy, or paying a debt consolidation company to consolidate your past due accounts that are in collection to aid you in paying off your past due accounts so that you can have financial stability later in life and enjoy the materialistic things of life. On an upscale, if you're tired of paying your mortgage, you can refinance your home at a lower interest rate and purchase another home with the cash and rent it out to the public for a two year lease, if you can find good tenants who will take care of your property. The monies from the lease can double as a payment for your home and now the $500 to $1,000 per month that you were paying for your mortgage can be used for savings or to purchase that new mustang or those Louboutins and you're on your way to financial freedom. Keep in mind none of this is possible without good credit. Debt consolidators{ XE "Debt consolidators" } will normally consolidate your debt for about a third of what you owe and in your mind. That $30,000 dollar debt being squashed to $10,000 feels like relief. And the $3,000 dollar fee these debt consolidators charge you for consolidating your debt doesn't sound like much huh. After reading this book, you will be able to do what debt consolidators have being doing for years and you will learn how to step by step build back up your credit, litigate and file civil lawsuits on your behalf without an attorney and become your own debt consolidator and clear your credit report while raising your score. Not only have I cleared credit reports with these legal platforms but I have won settlements against companies without filing suit in federal court. What you are about to learn is something that most attorneys will not show you. Why, when they receive upwards of $10,000 or more to litigate against debt collectors for unauthorized inquiries into your credit report or from deceptive means to collect debts. In the case of Trent v Bonewicz United States District court for the central division of Illinois 2013 U.S. Dist Lexis 3506, appeal no. 11-3332, decided January 9, 2013 attorneys were awarded $9,700 in actual attorney fees and the plaintiff was awarded $1,000 in actual damages based on the FDCPA (Fair Debt Collection Practices Act{ XE "Fair Debt Collection Practices Act" }) which we will go in depth with later and evaluate, based on the (FCRA{ XE "CRA" }) Fair Credit Reporting Act in which we will also discuss later. According to the 2013 Consumer Law Attorney Fee Survey Report, the average rate for consumer protection attorneys are 263 per hour for attorney's practicing 3 to 5 years and 430 per hour for attorney's practicing 11 to 15 years. A Pro Se litigant (you) can earn upwards of $115 per hour. But, first thing is first. You don t even know what the attorney fees are for and what the FCRA and the FDCPA really is. Now I will give you a step by step analysis on a way to financial freedom done right in the living room of your home.

CHAPTER 2: Obtaining Your Credit Report

Before you can learn about litigating claims for unauthorized inquiries on your credit report{ XE "credit report" } or removing delinquent accounts{ XE "delinquent accounts" } from your report, you must first learn the first step. Securing a credit report. (1) The first step into inquiring a credit report is to fill out the application at www.annualcreditreport.com{ XE "www.annualcreditreport.com" } which can be downloaded free from the site or you can write them and request for a credit report application at:

Annual Credit Request Service

P.O. Box 105281

Atlanta, Georgia 30348-5281

See example of credit application or tear the application from this book, make a copy and mail to the address above along with two forms of I.D.

EQUIFAX   **experian**   **TransUnion**

Annual Credit Report Request Form

You have the right to get a free copy of your credit file disclosure, commonly called a credit report, once every 12 months, from each of the nationwide consumer credit reporting companies - Equifax, Experian and TransUnion.

For instant access to your free credit report, visit www.annualcreditreport.com.

For more information on obtaining your free credit report, visit www.annualcreditreport.com or call 877-322-8228.

Use this form if you prefer to write to request your credit report from any, or all, of the nationwide consumer credit reporting companies. The following information is required to process your request. **Omission of any information may delay your request.**

Once complete, fold (do not staple or tape), place into a #10 envelope, affix required postage and mail to:

Annual Credit Report Request Service P.O. Box 105281 Atlanta, GA 30348-5281.

Please use a Black or Blue Pen and write your responses in PRINTED CAPITAL LETTERS without touching the sides of the boxes like the examples listed below:

A B C D E F G H I J K L M N O P Q R S T U V W X Y Z   0 1 2 3 4 5 6 7 8 9

Social Security Number: **Date of Birth:**

☐☐☐ - ☐☐ - ☐☐☐☐   ☐☐ / ☐☐ / ☐☐☐☐
                                          Month   Day   Year

Fold Here   Fold Here

First Name   **M.I.**

Last Name   **JR, SR, III, etc.**

Current Mailing Address:

House Number   **Street Name**

Apartment Number / Private Mailbox   **For Puerto Rico Only: Print Urbanization Name**

City   **State   ZipCode**

Previous Mailing Address (complete only if at current mailing address for less than two years):

House Number   **Street Name**

Fold Here   Fold Here

Apartment Number / Private Mailbox   **For Puerto Rico Only: Print Urbanization Name**

City   **State   ZipCode**

Shade Circle Like This → ●

Not Like This → ⊗ ⊘

I want a credit report from (shade each that you would like to receive):
○ Equifax
○ Experian
○ TransUnion

○ Shade here if, for security reasons, you want your credit report to include no more than the last four digits of your Social Security Number.

If additional information is needed to process your request, the consumer credit reporting company will contact you by mail.

Your request will be processed within 15 days of receipt and then mailed to you.

Copyright 2004, Central Source LLC

31238

Examples of Identification that may be accepted for obtaining a credit report{ XE "credit report" } are

- Utility Bill
- A Drivers license (not expired) (valid)
- Bank or credit union statement
- cancelled check
- signed homeless shelter check
- stamped post box office receipt
- Government issued I.D.
- State I.D. Card
- Pay Stub

For proof of Social Security number please provide:

- Social Security Card
- Letter from the Social Security Administration
- Military I.D.
- Medicaid or Medicare card
- Birth Certificate{ XE "Birth Certificate" }
- Government issued I.D.
- Passport

Important notes regarding acceptable forms of proof:

Utility bills, bank or credit union statements, cancelled checks, and pay stubs must be older than 2 months, P.O. Box receipts and homeless shelters must not be older than 12 months.

Within two weeks after mailing off your report (note: downloading is immediate) you will notice delinquencies on your report and some of them you will not be able to recognize, such as phone bills, cable bills, and other purchases your information was used for to obtain credit for and that's not the worse part of it all. The debt has been purchased by debt collectors who will harass you until they reach the goal of garnishing your wages.

Account Review Inquiries
FACTACT FREE DISCLOSURE POBox 1000, Chester, PA 19022 (800) 888-4213 Requested on 07/16/2003
REVENUE RECOVERY CORP 612 S Gay Street – 3$^{rd.}$ POBox 2698, Knoxville, TN 37901 (865) 971-1300 Requested on 05/22/2013
ALLSTATE 1819 Electric Road, Roanoke, VA 24018 (800) 255-7828 Requested on 06/16/2013
T-MOBILE 12920 SE 38th Street, Belleview, WA 98006 (800) 937-8997 Requested on 04/09/2013
GEICO INS CO One Geico Blvd., Fredericksburg, VA 22412 Requested on 05/22/2012

Every time someone makes an inquiry into your credit report{ XE "credit report" } your credit score lowers and unfortunately these unpaid bills that were sold to the debt collectors have caused a dramatic decrease into your credit score. Now there is some agency calling your phone from a blocked number claiming; that you owe a past due balance for a blockbuster rental that you failed to return and the store charged you $130 for a $9.99 movie and yes, this unpaid bill, once in collection and reported to the Big Three will lower your score. Did you know that pursuant to Title 15 of the United States Code that you can dispute{ XE "dispute" } the unpaid balance or debt and if the debt collector or agency that is trying to collect from you cannot provide the following:

- A copy of the original credit application showing the terms of the agreement.
- A summary of all activities, including all payments made, late charges, interest, and date of payments received, date of payments posted, charges made, and date of charges posted.
- Copies of all charge slips, invoices, promissory notes, and other documents proving indebtedness.
- Copies of all documents and financial instruments used to pay the disputed late payments.
- Copies of all documents sent to you regarding your account.

If these companies or debt collection agencies cannot produce these documents than you have no obligation to pay and they will try to resolve the dispute{ XE "dispute" } by sending a letter stating, "We have received your dispute. Our records indicate that you do owe us a past due balance but we will remove the alleged debt from your credit report{ XE "credit report" } and we will agree not to pursue civil action against you." Even though they may still claim you owe them. This is a win, because you have cleared this negative inquiry from your report and your credit rating now starts to elevate.

This practice of Title 15 1666 is called validating your debt and showing indebtedness. Sounds crazy huh? No, debt consolidation companies have been doing this for years and what they cannot remove. They will work out an agreement with the company for a lesser amount, sue the company without your awareness because you signed over a power of attorney for these consolidators to handle your indebtedness, and add it to your fee. Luckily for you I will show you step by step these procedures to do it yourself.

Pursuant to 1692 (e): A debt collector violates the Federal Debt Collection Practices Act when the debt collector threatens to take action that cannot be legally taken. "Well, Mr. Boyd I owe these people. I did get a cell phone and defaulted on the bill and never paid it." You may have, but these companies pursuant to title 15 1666 must show your   indebtedness and by not producing these documents because these companies kept bad records. You don't owe them a penny and even if you do. They cannot report it to the credit bureau and your credit score will not lower. Note: You may protect the unlawful use of your personal information by another person by placing a security freeze on your credit report{ XE "credit report" } (check local and state laws for proper procedures). However pursuant to the policy of Equifax, consumers who are not victims of identity theft may place a security freeze on their Equifax credit file. A security Freeze on your credit report will prohibit a credit reporting agency from releasing your credit report without your express authorization. The security freeze is designed to prevent a credit reporting agency from releasing your credit report without your consent. However you should be aware that using a security freeze to take control over who is allowed access to the personal and financial information in your credit report may delay and inference or prohibit the timely approval of any subsequent request or application you may make regarding a loan, credit, mortgage, government services, cellular telephones, utilities, internet credit, credit card transactions or other services, etc. When you place a freeze on your credit report you will be provided a personal identification number or password to authorize the temporary release of your credit report for a specific period. Note that placing a security freeze on your credit report will not stop a creditor or debt collector from placing an inquiry into your report or reporting delinquent accounts{ XE "delinquent accounts" }.

In the next chapter before I show you the step by step analysis into disputing debts, I will give you an overview of what the Fair Credit Reporting Act really means and a list of definitions that will be used in the litigating process so that you won't look like an amateur.

CHAPTER 3: Getting Started on Your Complaint

Now that you are familiar with why you will need good credit, it is time to learn 'what the FCRA (Fair Credit Reporting Act) really is and what it stands for.

The FCRA ,which comes from the Consumer Credit Reporting Reform Act of 1996 Pub. L. No. 204-208, 110 Stat. 3009 (1996), was enacted in 1996 to allow FCRA and FDCPA (Fair Debt Collection Practices Act{ XE "Fair Debt Collection Practices Act" }) to be brought into action in any appropriate U.S. District Court in regards of the controversy. The FCRA imposes civil liability for improper use and dissemination of credit information by a consumer reporting agency or user of reported information who willfully or negligently violates the Act see Rush v Macy's New York Inc. 775 F.2d 1554, 1557 11th cir 1985. Such liability may be imposed on users of information to obtain credit reports of consumers for purposes not specified in §1681b see Hinkle v CBE group 2012 U.S. Dist Lexis 26545, 2012 WL 681468 (S.D. 2012). What this all means is that in accordance with the FCRA, a company cannot post your credit report{ XE "credit report" } online for others to see or make a non-purpose pull of your credit report for review without certain factors. Before we go into filing lawsuits or civil complaint{ XE "civil complaint" }s, let's start with definitions that you need to know in order to be successful and remove your past due collections, bills, etc., from your report.

Consumer{ XE "Consumer" } - The definition of a consumer within the meaning of FCRA 15 U.S.C. §1681a(c) describes the plaintiff which is you.

Corporation{ XE "Corporation" } -The definition of a "corporation" within the meaning of FCRA 15 U.S.C. §1681a (b) describes the defendant-the company who you are disputing.

Consumer Report{ XE "Consumer Report" } - the FCRA defines a consumer report as any written, oral, or other communication of any information by a consumer reporting agency bearing on a consumer's credit worthiness, credit standing, credit capacity, character, general reputation, personal character, or mode of living which is used or expected to be used or collection whole or in part for the purpose of serving as a factor in establishing the consumer's eligibility for credit or insurance, employment purposes, or any other purpose authorized under §1681b.

§1681b(f){ XE "§1681b(f)" } prohibits users from impermissibly obtaining or using consumer reports.

§15 U.S.C. § 1681 (8){ XE "§15 U.S.C. § 1681 (8)" } - A credit bureau must provide a consumer or plaintiff with a credit report{ XE "credit report" }.

§1681a(c){ XE "§1681a(c)" } - consumer statue

§1681a(b){ XE "§1681a(b)" } - corporation statue

§1681{ XE "§1681" }- Fair Credit Reporting Act

15 U.S.C. §1692{ XE "15 U.S.C. §1692" } - Fair Debt Collection Practices Act{ XE "Fair Debt Collection Practices Act" }

15 U.S.C. §1681p{ XE "15 U.S.C. §1681p" } - Jurisdiction of the court is conferred by this statue.

15 U.S.C. § 139lb{ XE "15 U.S.C. § 139lb" } -Venue is proper in the circuit court pursuant to this statue.

§1681n{ XE "§1681n" } - statutory damages of $1,000.00 §1692a (6)-definition of a debt collector

§1692 (e){ XE "§1692 (e)" } -definition of a false representation of the amount

§ 1692(e){ XE "§ 1692(e)" } - A debt collector violates the debt collection act when he threatens to take action that cannot be legally taken pursuant to 15 U.S.C. 1666.

§1692e(30){ XE "§1692e(30)" } - represents the judgment.

Reasons to pull credit{ XE "Reasons to pull credit" }-Applying for credit with the company (2) services (3) employment or insurance.

Rule 68{ XE "Rule 68" } - Rule 68 prompts parties to a suit to evaluate the risks and costs of litigation and to balance them against the likelihood of success upon trial on the merits. Rule 68 allows a defendant to make a firm, non-negotiable offer of judgment offer and plaintiff may accept or refuse the offer.

Purpose of a Rule 68 offer{ XE "Purpose of a Rule 68 offer" } -The purpose is to encourage settlement and avoid litigation inside a United States District Court see Marek v Chesney 473 U.S. 1,7 (1985).

Tacit agreement{ XE "Tacit agreement" } - The definition of a tacit agreement is an agreement from a silent party.

> Example - you file a request to show indebtedness from a company that has provided an inquiry on your report which states that you owe them a balance. If they do not respond to your letter(s) then the agreement is tacit so whatever you are saying is the truth.

Pintos analysis{ XE "Pintos analysis" } - Pintos v Pac Creditors Ass'n 605 F.3d 665,678 9th cir 2010- A debt collector within 5 years after the initial communication with a consumer to send the ~

consumer a written notice contrary to certain information.

Article III{ XE "Article III" } - The definition of article III requests plaintiffs to establish three things (1) injury (2) causation (3) redressibility.

Causation{ XE "Causation" } - The causing or producing of an effect.

Redressibility{ XE "edressibility" } - A means of seeking relief or remedy-if the statue of limitations has run. The plaintiff is without redress. (2) Relief, money damages as opposed to equitable relief, is the only redress available.

injury{ XE "injury" }- The violation of another's legal right, for which the law provides a remedy, a wrong or injustice (2) Anything done or said in breach of duty not to do it, if harm results to another in person, character, or property (3) Any harm or damage-may be criminal or civil.

Statute of limitations{ XE "Statute of limitations" } - A law that bars claims after a specified period. A statue establishing a time limit for suing in a civil case, based on the date when the claim accrued (as when the injury occurred or was discovered). The purpose of the statue is to require diligent prosecution of known claims.

Forma Pauperis{ XE "Forma Pauperis" } -To proceed without

paying fees

§1681 (a)(3)(A){ XE "§1681 (a)(3)(A)" } - A collection agency is permitted to obtain a consumer report if the agency is doing so for the purpose of collecting a debt.

§1681b (c)(1){ XE "§1681b (c)(1)" } - under this statue a credit reporting agency (CRA{ XE "CRA" }) may provide a consumer report information about a consumer to a user or company who will make a firm offer of credit to the consumer.

§1681b(c){ XE "§1681b(c)" } - governs the use of prescreened consumer report information and specifically provides that a consumer reporting agency may furnish a consumer report relating to any consumer in connection with any credit or insurance transaction that is not initiated by the consumer if the consumer authorizes the agency to provide such report to such person or the transaction consists of a firm offer of credit or insurance.

Big Three Credit Bureaus and Addresses:

- Equifax Inc.
  P.O. box 740123
  Atlanta, GA 30374-0123

- Consumer Financial Protection Bureau
  POBox 4503
  Iowa City, IA 52244

- Experian
  P.O. Box 919
  Allen, TX 75013

- Transunion
  P.O. Box 505
  Woodlyn, PA 19094

- Federal Trade Commission
  Consumer Response Center
  Washington D.C. 20580
  Phone 1-877-382-4357

30 days{ XE "30 days" } - Time limitation once a consumer receives a credit report{ XE "credit report" } to attack or dispute{ XE "dispute" } impermissible pull, inquiry, or debt.

Hard pull{ XE "Hard pull" } - A hard pull is a full credit inquiry conducted when someone applies for a loan or line of credit. It may lower a score see Herkins Jr. v Diversified Services Inc. no. PJM 12-1229 2012 U.S. Dist Lexis 166963 2012 WL 5928997 at 1 (Maryland 2012).

Soft pull{ XE "Soft pull" } - is a request for updated information see Norman v RJM Acquisitions LLC no. 3:11-cv-1330-D-2012 U.S. Dist Lexis 1113338, 2012 WL 3204977at 1.

Permissible Pull{ XE "Permissible Pull" } - A reason to obtain a consumer's credit report{ XE "credit report" } based on consumer owing of a debt or consumer applied for insurance, credit, etc. etc.

21

Non-permissible pull{ XE "Non-permissible pull" } - unauthorized pull of a consumer's credit report{ XE "credit report" }.

Supplemental Income{ XE "Supplemental Income" } - Income that is considered to be extra income after all bills and necessities are paid.

Badeker v Midland Credit management 2012 U.S. Dist Lexis 169645-Pro Se motion where Forma Pauperis{ XE "Forma Pauperis" } was granted to pursue a FCRA or FDCPA claim (remember Forma Pauperis means to proceed without paying the filing fee. (Note: there is no filing fee when disputing debts.) The disputes are mailed to the big three or the company.

$350.00 dollars - filing fee{ XE "filing fee" } for filing FDCPA and FCRA claims in federal Court.

15 U.S.C. §1692a(6){ XE "15 U.S.C. §1692a(6)" } - Any creditor who in the process of collecting his own debts, uses any name other than his own which would indicate that a third person is collecting or attempting to collect such debts is considered a debt collector.

15 U.S.C. § 1692e (4){ XE "15 U.S.C. § 1692e (4)" } - The FDCPA also prohibits communication that implies that non-payment of a debt will result in the garnishment or sale of unless such action is lawful (proof under title 15 1566 of indebtedness, not just because you owe them makes it lawful, they must have the records) and the debt

collector intends to take such action.

The FDCPA{ XE "FDCPA" } - (Fair Debt Collection Practices Act{ XE "Fair Debt Collection Practices Act" })- Prohibits causing a telephone to ring or engaging in a telephone conversation repeating about the debt with the intent to annoy, abuse, or harass any person other than the called number.

15 U.S.C. § 16810(a){ XE "15 U.S.C. § 16810(a)" } - If a violation of the FCRA is negligent than a plaintiff is entitled to actual damages. (Meaning non-compliance) if willful than a plaintiff is entitled to statutory damages, actual damages, and punitive damages, (meaning you mailed them the dispute{ XE "dispute" } and they failed to remove the item or the collection after they responded to you without proof only a validation of your address that you owed them).

Types of conduct that are a violation –

1. The use of violence or other criminal means too harm the physical and reputation of the person.
2. The use of profane language.
3. The publication of a list of consumers who allegedly refused to pay debts, except for a consumer reporting agency or persons meeting the requirements of section 603(f) or 604(3) of this act.
4. The advertising of sale of any debt to coerce payment of the

debt

15 U.S.C. 1692 c(c){ XE "15 U.S.C. 1692 c(c)" } - Notifying a debt collector by a cease and desist payment dispute{ XE "dispute" } letter in respect to the debt.

Title 15 U.S.C. §168ic (a) (6){ XE "Title 15 U.S.C. §168ic (a) (6)" } - a consumer reporting agency shall not furnish for employment purposes or in connection with a credit transaction a consumer report that contains medical information.

Title 15 U.S.C. § 1681k{ XE "Title 15 U.S.C. § 1681k" } - a consumer reporting agency shall not finish investigative report that includes information that is a matter of public record that relates to an arrest, an indictment, civil action, or outstanding judgment.

Title 15 U.S.C. § i681g{ XE "Title 15 U.S.C. § i681g" } - If the consumer to the file requests that the first 5 digits of the social security number be removed from disclosure this subsection covers this section. Title 15 U.S.C. §1681e (e)(l) - describes a person that has procured a consumer report.

Home Loan Applicant{ XE "Home Loan Applicant" } - the lender must disclose to you the score that a consumer reporting agency distributed to users and the lender used in connection with your home loan Title 15 U.S.C. § 1681 j-statue that once during any 12 month request period a CRA{ XE "CRA" } shall provide a free report, see also 1581a.

Title 15 U.S.C. § 1681r{ XE "Title 15 U.S.C. § 1681r" } - any officer or employee of a CRA{ XE "CRA" } who knowingly and willfully provides information concerning an individual from the agency shall be fined under Title 18 and imprisoned for 2 years.

Title 15 U.S.C. § 1681s-2{ XE "Title 15 U.S.C. § 1681s-2" } - a furnisher{ XE "furnisher" } must provide notice of dispute{ XE "dispute" } to CRA{ XE "CRA" }-notice of closed accounts, notice of delinquency of accounts, a consumer may dispute the debt directly with a furnisher based on the Federal trade Commission and the National Credit Union Administration.

Title 15 U.S.C. §{ XE "Title 15 U.S.C. §" } - Statue for duties of furnishers of information upon notice of dispute{ XE "dispute" } A. conduct an investigation of the disputed information review all relevant information provided by the consumer B report the results to the Bureau. If any item is inaccurate or complete and cannot be verified by Title 15 1666 the furnisher{ XE "furnisher" } must modify the item, delete, the item, or permanently block the reporting of that item.

Title 15 § I67d{ XE "Title 15 § I67d" } - Credit Repair organizations.{ XE "Credit Repair organizations." }

Title 15 U.S.C. 1673{ XE "Title 15 U.S.C. 1673" } Restriction on garnishment{ XE "Restriction on garnishment" } 25 percentage of his or her disposable earnings for that week or if it exceeded 30 times the amount of minimum hourly wage

Title 15 U.S.C. 1692b{ XE "Title 15 U.S.C. 1692b" } - Any debt collector communicating with any person other than the consumer for the purpose of acquiring location information about the consumer shall identify himself, state that he is confirming or correcting location information concerning the consumer and only if expressly requested identify his employer.

1. Not state that such a consumer owes any debt.
2. Not communicate with any such person more than once unless requested to do so by such person or unless the debt collector reasonably believes that the earlier response of such person is erroneous or incomplete and that such person now has correct or complete location information.
3. Not communicate by post card
4. Not use any language or symbol on any envelope or in the contents of any communication affected by the mails or telegram that indicates that the debt collector is in debt collection business or that the communication relates to the collection of a debt,

Without the prior permission or consent of the consumer given directly to the debt collector or the express permission of a court of competent jurisdiction. A debt collector may not communicate with a consumer in connection with the collection of any debt.

Ceasing communication{ XE "Ceasing communication" } - If a consumer notifies a debt collector in writing that the consumer refuses to pay a debt or that the consumer wishes the debt collector cease further communication. The debt collector shall not communicate based on such debt.

Venue{ XE "Venue" } - Any debt collector who brings any legal action on a debt against any consumer shall bring the action in the judicial District in which such consumer signed the contract or where the consumer resides.

Title 15 U.S.C. 692b{ XE "15 U.S.C. 692b" } any debt collector communicating with any person other than the consumer for the purpose of acquiring location about the consumer shall identify himself not state that such consumer owes any debt.

Validation of debts{ XE "Validation of debts" } Title 15 1692g{ XE "Title 15 1692g" } - Within five days after the initial communication with a consumer in connection with a debt. A debt collector shall send a written notice of the amount of the debt (2) the name of the creditor to whom the debt is owed (3) a statement that unless the consumer within 30 days after the receipt of the notice disputes the validity of the debt.

Disputed debts{ XE "Disputed debts" } - If the consumer notifies the debt collector in writing within the thirty day period that the debt or any portion thereof is disputed, the debt collector shall cease collection of the debt until the debt collector obtains verification of the debt pursuant to title 15 section 1666{ XE "title 15 section 1666" }.

Admission of liability{ XE "Admission of liability" } - The failure of a consumer to dispute{ XE "dispute" } the validity of the debt under this section may not be construed by any court as an admission of liability by the consumer. Notice provisions-The sending or delivery of any form any form or notice which does not relate to the collection of a debt and is expressly required by the Internal Revenue Code of 1986

Title 15 U.S.C. 1692h{ XE "Title 15 U.S.C. 1692h" } - if a consumer owes multiple debts and makes a single payment to any debt collector with respect to other debts. A debt collector may not apply the payment to other debts.

Title 15 U.S.C. 1692j{ XE "Title 15 U.S.C. 1692j" } - It is unlawful to design, compile, and furnish any form knowing that such form would be used to create the false belief in a consumer that a person other than the creditor of such consumer is participating in the collection of or in attempt to collect a debt that consumer owes.

Title 15 U.S.C. 1692p{ XE "Title 15 U.S.C. 1692p" } - This code is an exception for certain bad check enforcement programs by private entities. A private entity shall be excluded from the definition of a debt collector.

Bad Check violation{ XE "Bad Check violation" } - means a violation of the applicable state criminal law relating to the writing of dishonored checks.

Title 15 U.S.C. 1692i{ XE "Title 15 U.S.C. 1692i" } - Any debt collector who brings legal action on a debt against a consumer.

Title 15 U.S.C. § 1692{ XE "Title 15 U.S.C. § 1692" } – Whenever a consumer reporting agency prepares an investigative consumer report, no adverse information way be included.

Title 15 U.S.C. 1681s{ XE "Title 15 U.S.C. 1681s" } – 1 - Statue on overdue child support obligations exceptions do not apply to Chapter 13 of Title 11 of the U.S. Code or any debt due to State or federal tax.

Title 15 U.S.C. § 1674{ XE "Title 15 U.S.C. § 1674" } - Termination of employment may not be governed for garnishment of wages or civil liability is forced on the employer for $1,000 and more than one year in prison

Consumer Reporting Agency{ XE "Consumer Reporting Agency" } §1681 k (f){ XE "§1681 k (f)" } - Prohibits users from impermissibly obtaining or using consumer reports Title 15 U.S.C. § 1679b - No credit repair organization .may charge or receive any money or other valuable consideration for the performance of any services which the credit repair organization has agreed to perform for any consumer before such service is fully performed.

Title Section 1666{ XE "Title Section 1666" } governs the correction of billing errors. This title again prevents action by creditors to collect amount of any part regarded as a billing error.

Title 15 U.S.C. § 1681 c-2{ XE "Title 15 U.S.C. § 1681 c-2" } - no person shall sell, transfer for consideration, or place a debt that such person has been notified to be under identity theft.

Title 15 U.S.C. § I681p{ XE "Title 15 U.S.C. § I681p" } - An action may be brought in the U.S. District Court in nature of an amount in controversy not later than:

1. Two years after the date of discovery by the plaintiff for the violation that is the basis for such liability; or
2. Five years after the date on which the violation that is the basis for such liability occurs.

Lodestar{ XE "Lodestar" } - A reasonable amount of attorney fees in a given case, calculated by multiplying reasonable number of hours worked by the prevailing hourly rate in the community for similar work and often considering such additional factors as the decree of :

skill and difficulty involved in the case, the degree of its urgency, its novelty, and like. Most statues that award attorney fees use the lodestar method.

Validate - Legally sufficient binding contract, meritorious claim or conclusion based on the facts, evidence of the debt.

Title 15 U.S.C. § 1692(g)(4) – validation of debt.

Title 15 U.S.C. § 1601 – timely written notice that a dispute is being filed to decline and not pay the debt.

1692(f) – The use of unfair and unconscionable means to collect the alleged debt.

Floating loan – A credit infusion from the bank to purchase items by writing checks. No cash infusions or bank withdraws are available.

Title 15 §1666(a) – any creditor who fails to comply with section 162 U.S.C. § 1666(a) forfeits right to collect.

Robert Boyd

CHAPTER 4: Receiving Your Credit Reports

Now that you have received your credit report{ XE "credit report" } and you have learned of the outstanding balances. The common question is what do I do from here. You will now do what debt consolidators have been charging you for. You will begin to dispute{ XE "dispute" } the old accounts.[Note that dispute is defined in the Webster's American Thesaurus as: argue, debate, controversy, argumentation, or conflict.] Meaning in common average every day terms as a misunderstanding of principle or balance. [Note that once you receive your credit report there is only a 30 day gap to file a dispute with one of the Big Three Reporting Agencies - Experian, Equifax, or Transunion in which the Bureau will conduct an investigation in which we will discuss inside the next chapter.]

Robert Boyd

CHAPTER 5: Disputing the Credit Debts

NOW that you have studied the definitions and have a minimal idea of what you are about to do and what the FCRA means and stands for. It's time to dispute{ XE "dispute" } the debts on your credit report{ XE "credit report" }. Now there are two ways to dispute the credit report.

The most common way is through the credit Bureau. The FCRA has placed a limited sanction of laws on CRA{ XE "CRA" }-Credit Reporting Agencies for not following through with reasonable investigative means to ensure that the debt is owed pursuant to Title 15 U.S.C. 15 1666 known as 15 U.S.C. §1581e (b). The CRA must follow reasonable procedures to ensure maximum accuracy of their information condemning the individual about what the report relates to. When a CRA fails to comply with these restraints. A violation of statue 15 U.S.C. §1581 has occurred because the CRA failed to investigate the consumer's or plaintiff's credit file without determining whether those companies has a permissible pull to obtain that credit file or to report a debt owed. Pursuant to 15 U.S.C. §1681s- 2(b) the CRA must conduct a reasonable investigation into plaintiff's credit dispute{ XE "dispute" }.

See Miller v Equifax 2012 U.S. Dist Lexis 168894 3:ll-cv-012 where Equifax was held liable for failing to follow reasonable procedures to ensure the accuracy of the information. Accuracy of information may be based on the company showing or proving   indebtedness based on title 15 1666. This is also called a verification of the alleged debt. Most companies will trick you into thinking that a verification of debt is only a file or letter showing you a balance of the alleged debt. No, this is not sufficient. Let's go back to Title 15 1666. A company must show you:

1. A copy of the original credit application showing the terms of the agreement; and
2. A summary of all activities, including late payments made, late charges, interest, date of payments received, date of payments posted, copies of all documents and financial instruments, copies of all charge slips, invoices, promissory notes, and other documents proving indebtedness.

If the company does not show you this information, you will need the help of the Federal Trade Commission. This is done easily by writing them a letter and sending copies of all letters you have mailed to the company to dispute{ XE "dispute" } the debt. This is also the Second prong in disputing the debt. Attacking the lender or the debt collector. Now that you have learned of the two ways to dispute the debt. Let's start you off with a step by step analysis of disputing your debts using the first analysis of the Credit Bureau. It's simply done by filling in the blanks below-see sample. These exhibits are normally found inside your credit report{ XE "credit report" } once you receive the report. See Below

---

DISPUTE FORM

This Form is being provided as a simplified means of communicating legitimate disputes only. By no means should accurate, valid and verifiable information be disputed.

STEPS TO DISPUTE THE ACCURACY OF ANY ITEM ON YOUR CREDIT REPORT:

PLEASE READ "IMPORTANT INFORMATION"

- Fill out this Dispute Form completely; supply photocopies of all proof of payment and/or documentation.
- If you dispute information from more than one agency, you must dispute the information directly with them.
- If your identifying information differs from the information listed on the credit report. A photocopy of your driver's license, social Security card & a recent utility bill will help the Credit Reporting Agency expedite the reinvestigation.
- Keep a photocopy of all information mailed to the Credit Reporting Agencies for your records.

PLEASE USE A SEPARATE DISPUTE FORM FOR EACH CREDIT REPORTING AGENCY

Last Name _____ First Name _____ Middle Initial _____ Jr, Sr, II, III, IV _____

Address _____ Social Security Number _____

City _____ State _____ Zip Code _____ Date of Birth _____

Previous Address _____ City _____ State _____ Zip _____

DISPUTED ACCOUNT INFORMATION

1. Company Name _____ 3. Company Name _____
Account # _____ Account # _____
Not my account _____ Never paid late _____ Not my account _____ Never paid late _____
Included in Bankruptcy _____ Paid in full _____ Included in Bankruptcy _____ Paid in full _____
Other: (please explain) _____ Other: (please explain) _____

2. Company Name _____ 4. Company Name _____
Account # _____ Account # _____
Not my account _____ Never paid late _____ Not my account _____ Never paid late _____
Included in Bankruptcy _____ Paid in full _____ Included in Bankruptcy _____ Paid in full _____
Other: (please explain) _____ Other: (please explain) _____

At your request, The Credit Reporting Agency will send the results of the reinvestigation to organizations who have reviewed your credit report within the past 6 months (12 months for Colorado, New York and Maryland residents) and/or employers who have required within the past two years. Please list the organization you would like notified, using the space below.

SIGNATURE _____ DATE _____

Complete this form & mail to Equifax, For Experian & TransUnion please visit their website to file a dispute online.

Experian	**Equifax**	**TransUnion**
www.experian.com/rs/fl3.8.html	Consumer Disputes	www.TransUnion.com
PO Box 2002	PO Box 740256	2 Baldwin Place
Allen, TX 75013	Atlanta, GA 30374-0256	PO Box 1000
888-397-3742	By Mail Only	Chester, PA 19022-2000
		800-888-4213

Like I said before, there are two ways to dispute{ XE "dispute" } your credit report{ XE "credit report" }. The second step and most effective is disputing the credit report from the lender analysis. In the next chapter you will find the methods for disputing the debt accounts and balances by using the samples I have provided for you that are guaranteed to work.

Chapter 6: Disputing From the Credit Bureau Analysis & the Lender or Debt Collector Analysis

As I have explained to you before, there are two ways of disputing balances of debts and late payments on your credit report{ XE "credit report" }. One effective analysis is from the Credit Bureau analysis which is the most common. As you can see on page 35. This dispute{ XE "dispute" } format is found inside your credit report. Not mines in the credit reporting world defined when you are disputing debt means that the report is inaccurate because the outstanding balance could not have been done by you because you were either out of the country, in prison, out of state, at work during the time of the credit application or in the hospital, etc. Or maybe you are a Junior and your father is a Senior and the furnisher{ XE "furnisher" } reported the debt to the wrong person. Either way pursuant to Title 15 Section 1666, the lender or debt collector attempting to collect the debt must be able to show a signed application with either your signature or the other requirements of Title 15 Section 1666. The next example that you will find is a typed Dispute that may serve as a format for disputing with the Credit

Bureau. Please note that based on the FCRA. The Credit Bureau has 60 days to complete their investigation. Within 60 days you should receive a letter stating that the outstanding balances that are lowering your credit score have been removed or the letter may state that the inaccuracy is accurate and you still owe the balance to the lender. This is where your skills will come into play after reading this book. Sometimes the Credit Bureau like any company with employees fail to hold these furnishers or debt collectors who are stating you owe this debt to their correct procedures to show indebtedness. The next sample letter is a letter requesting for the Credit Bureau to describe their investigation procedures used to determine your indebtedness to those companies or lenders who have reported your outstanding bills to the credit Bureau. The 3rd and final sample is a sample letter to the Credit Bureau stating that the furnisher who has reported a late payment to the Credit Bureau has provided inaccurate information and sometimes these companies do so accidently. Remember any employee is capable of a mistake. It is up to you to find those mistakes. Whenever a company cannot show indebtedness based on Title 15 Section 1666. Then you do not owe them a thing and if the credit Bureau fails to do their proper investigative procedures. You may hold them liable for civil penalties up to 1,000 dollars in statutory damages in which we will discuss later.

The other format into disputing debt is the analysis of disputing the debt from the lender side{ XE "lender side" } who sometimes collect the debt outsourced through debt collectors who also may purchase the debt at a lower fee or rate from the lender and charge you hidden fees when they are attempting to collect the debt. The lender side works the same as the credit Bureau side except this time instead of sending a letter to one of the three Big three companies. You mail the dispute{ XE "dispute" } letter(s) to the lenders or debt collectors see samples.

After 30 days if there is no communication then the company to whom you are in dispute{ XE "dispute" } with has formed a tacit agreement with you by their silence see sample.

The next step is to mail a dispute{ XE "dispute" } letter stating that the company has failed to rebut what your dispute has stated and normally this would cause the company or debt collector to remove the inaccurate debt from your credit report{ XE "credit report" }. If the company is not silent and responds that you are in debt to them. Mail a request as before of the evidence pursuant to title 15 section 1666{ XE "title 15 section 1666" } of the alleged debt. And to validate pursuant to 15 U.S.C. 1692(g)(4).

After 30 days if the company or debt collector cannot produce the records pursuant to Title 15 section 1666, then you do not owe them.

Robert Boyd

Credit Report

Credit Summary From 11/1/86 To 5/22/01

Public Records	3	Collections	4	Negative Trades	1
Hist Neg Trades	0	# Trades	1	Revolving	0
Hist Neg Occurr	0	Installment	0	Mortgage	0
Open Trades	1	Inquiries	3		

Type	High	Limit	Balance	Past Due	Payment	%Avail
Closed	$0	$0	$202	$202	$0	-
Totals	$0	$0	$202	$202	$0	-

Public Records

Reported/ Amount	ECOA/ Subscriber	Assets	Type/ Plaintiff/Attorney	Docket/ Paid	Court/ City, State
0X/95 984	C Z 0XXXXXX		Civil judgement Pltff: BXXXX MOTOR CO Attn: VXX P1	95CVM11X	Superior Court
0X/98	I Z 0XXXXXX		Chapter 7 bnkrptcy discharged Attn: THOMAS X HXXXX	9802XXX 0X/99	Federal District
0X/98 1903	I Z 0XXXXXX		Civil judgement Pltff: PETER RABBIT	21XXX	Common Pleas

Collection Accounts

Firm/ID Code ECOA	Paid/ CLSD	Placed/ CS(MOP)	VRFD/ BAL	$PLCD/	Acc#	Creditor Name	Remarks
ATTN L.L.C. Y 0XXXXXX1	I	05/99	05/00A O9B	83 83	8XXX	COLXXXX XXXXXXXXXX MEDICAL CENT	Placed for collection
CREDBURSYS Y 0XXXXXX1	I	09/98	03/00A O9B	216 216	22XXXXXXXXXX	XXXXXX HOSPITAL	Placed for collection
CREDBURSYS Y XXXXXXXX1	I	02/98	03/00A O9B	201 201	825XXXXX80	XXXXXX HOSPITAL	Placed for collection
CAP RCV SVC Y 0XXXXXX	I	07/94	07/96A O9B	57 57	2XXXX	FOOT XXXXX	Placed for collection

Open Accounts

Acc Name/Address	Rptd/ ECOA	Opened/ Clsd/PD	High/ Limit	Pmt/ Term	Bal	Past Due	Current Status Mths	30	60	90	Rating
S C ELEC/GAS 3XXXXXX5 Subscriber code: U 0XXXXX Loan Type: Utility Company Remarks: Account closed by consumer	03/99A I	07/96 02/97F	202		202	202					O09
Open Account Totals				$0	$202						

Dispute Letter sample 1

Certified mail number: _____

November 6, 2014

DMV Collection Services [Example]
111 Victory Park
Louisville, Kentucky 42136

Re: Dispute Letter to cease and desist or validate claim
[The reason for this action letter]
Account number: 785648290 [Account Number]

Dear: Lender or Collection Agency, whichever applies

Your company is currently reporting a negative listing to the three Credit Bureaus (Experian, Transunion, and Equifax) regarding the above reference account. Based on my records, I can find no reason for your firm to report such credit history. If you will review your records, I know that you will find your reported notations are inaccurate. 15 U.S.C. 1692(e) states a debt collector cannot take action unless the debt is validated under 15 U.S.C. 1692(g)(4).

The erroneous status of your credit reporting agency records are unacceptable and are preventing me from obtaining necessary financing. Pursuant to Title 15 Section 1666 of the United States Code. I formally request the following documentation evidence pertaining to my account:

- A copy of the original Application showing the terms of the agreement.
- A summary of all account activities, including all payments made, late charges, interest, date of payments received, date of payments posted, charges made, and date of charges posted.
- Copies of all documents and financial instruments used to pay

the disputed late payments not limited to cash or Bills of Exchange.

- Copies of all charge slips, invoices, promissory notes, and all other documents proving indebtedness.
- Copies of all documents sent to me regarding my account.
- Please evidence your authorization to do business in the state of (whatever state the debt collector is from).
- Please evidence your authorization pursuant to 15 U.S.C. 1992(3) and 15 U.S.C. 1992(f) in this alleged matter.
- What is your authorization of law for your collection in this matter?
- What is your authorization of law for your collection of this alleged debt?
- Please evidence your proof of this alleged debt including the contract or instrument bearing my signature.

This information and documentation is critical and time is of essence. Within less than 30 days, I will be damaged partially because of the discrepancy with your reported records. The above code requires your response within 30 days. Your attention to this notice will be greatly appreciated.

If you find that your documentation does not support the negative credit history reported to the Big Three Credit bureaus. Please submit a completed universal data form to the Bureaus in order to remove the negative notations and I will agree not to pursue statutory and punitive damages caused by this reported notation.

I can be reached at the address below.

Thank You.
[Your name]
[Your address]

Dispute Letter Late Payments

Robert Boyd
Address: 222 South Dixie Highway
Cave City, KY 42127

Certified mail number: _____

November 6, 2014

Creditor or Credit Bureau [name of company]
Address
City, State   Zip

Dear Creditor or Bureau: [choose one]

I recently received a credit report{ XE "credit report" } that appears to have errors. There are some late payments that are wrong, based on my recollection. Please correct the following:

Betters Days West:	#989798998	MO/Day/Year
Hip Hop Fashion:	#890738939	MO/Day/Year
First National Bank:	#89383939	MO/Day/Year
GE Eclectic:	#474849409	MO/Day/Year
		(Please include the dates)

I appreciate your attention to this. Please remove these errors or provide me with information that these records are accurate.

Thank You,
Robert Boyd
Social Security Number: 435-16-0719

Robert Boyd

<u>Dispute Sample Letter (Not Mine)</u>

Robert Boyd
222 South Dixie Highway
Cave City, Kentucky 42127

Certified mail number: _____

November 6, 2014

Creditor Name
Creditor Address
City, State   Zip

    RE: Cease and desist collection activities
        Account Number #_____

Dear Creditor, Credit Card Lender, Credit Lender:

I have recently received a copy of my credit report{ XE "credit report" }. The Equifax report had an account listed from your company as a credit card. I disputed the account with the Credit bureau as not mine but it recently came back as verified. In accordance with 15 U.S.C. 1692(e) and Title 15 1666, collection cannot be legally taken without a validation pursuant to 15 U.S.C. 1692(g)(4).

I am writing this letter to you in an effort to get this removed. Please delete your information from my credit report{ XE "credit report" }. I have never had an account - with your company. Someone has opened an account in my name; please close immediately before further harm is done.

I am requesting that you notify all of the credit bureaus that this account is disputed or that you delete this account until this matter is resolved. This is required by the Fair Credit Reporting Act.

If there is any paperwork that I need to sign to confirm that this account is not mine, please send me the required documents.

This is a written dispute{ XE "dispute" } of this account per the Fair Debt Reporting Act, the Fair Debt Collection Practices Act{ XE "Fair Debt Collection Practices Act" } and the Fair Credit Billing Act. Please be aware that I am exercising all my rights per these laws and all other applicable laws protecting them. In accordance with Title 15 U.S.C. 1666, I am requesting the original credit application with my signed signature showing the original terms of the agreement. Please evidence your authorization to do business in the state of _____. Failure to remove this alleged debt or to validate claim will lead to civil action pursuant to the FDCPA, Consumer Protection Act, and I will request a Rule 69 Offer of Judgment. If this item is not removed in ten days, I will file a claim with the FTC.

Thank You,
Robert Boyd
Social Security Number: 435-16-0719

Robert Boyd

Dispute Letter Step 2 if no response

Robert Boyd
222 South Dixie Highway
Cave City, KY 42127

Certified mail number: _____

November 6, 2014

Creditor Name
Creditor Address
City, State   Zip

> RE: Cease and desist collection activities
> Follow up to dispute{ XE "dispute" } letter
> Account Number #_____

Dear Creditor, Credit Card Lender, Credit Lender:

This letter shall serve as formal notice of my intent to file a complaint with the FTC Federal Trade Commission due to your blatant non-response and disregard of law.

As indicated by the attached copies of letter and mailing receipts (certified mail slips), you have received accepted through registered mail my dispute{ XE "dispute" } letter dated 3-25-79 (date you mailed the first letter). To date you have not done your duty as mandated by federal law and the FCRA. Your non-compliance with federal law is unacceptable and you must be held accountable.

Federal law requires you to respond within 30 days, yet you have failed to respond. Failure to comply with these federal regulations by credit reporting agencies are investigated by the Federal Trade Commission see 15 USC 41. I am maintaining a careful record of my communications with you on this matter, for the purpose of filing a complaint with the FTC should you continue with your non compliance. I further remind you that as in Wenger v Trans Union Corp no. 95- 6445 (1995) you may be liable for your non-compliance.

For the record, the following information is being erroneously included on my credit report{ XE "credit report" }, as I have advised you on two separate occasions, more than 60 days and again in 30 days.

Name of creditor or agency-account number: _____

If you do not immediately remove this inaccurate and incomplete information, I will file a formal complaint with the FTC should you continue to operate with complete disregard for the law, I intend to seek redress in civil suit for the recovery of damages, costs, and attorney fees. For this purpose I am documenting these events and letters, including the lack of non-response which serves as a tacit agreement with me and your firm that your records are insufficient and must be removed from my credit report{ XE "credit report" }. You are further directed to supply a corrected credit profile to all creditors who have received an erroneous report from your firm.

> Thank You,
> Robert Boyd
> Social Security Number: 435-16-0719

Robert Boyd

Dispute Letter 3

[Validate debt-This temporarily stops collection or garnish of wages]

Robert Boyd
222 South Dixie Highway
Cave City, KY 42127

Certified mail number: _____

November 6, 2014

Creditor or Debt Collector: MHRS Services
3350 Old Lexington Road
Paducah, Kentucky 23498

      Re: Cease and Desist Collection Activities
              Account #202106008712798
              Original creditor: Tribble Phone Services
              [Account Number /Original Creditor name]

Dear Sir or Madam:

Thank You for your recent inquiry. This is not a refusal to pay, but a notice that your claim is being disputed. This is a request for validation made pursuant to the Fair Debt Collection practices Act (FDCPA). Please be advised pursuant Title 15 section code 1666 if the following documents cannot be presented such as the original credit application bearing my signature, a summary of all account activities, including payments made, late charges, interest, date of payments posted, charge slips, all financial instruments used to pay the disputed debt and all documents regarding my account. My address is not a validation of debt. 15 U.S.C. 1692(e) states that a false, deceptive and misleading representation in connection with the collection of any debt includes the false representation of the character or legal status of any debt. It

50

further identifies as a deceptive practice any threat to take action that cannot legally be taken.

Please evidence your authorization pursuant to 15 U.S.C. 1692(e) and 15 U.S.C. 1692(f) in this alleged matter.
Please provide your authorization of law for your collection in this matter.
Please provide authorization of law to do business or operate in the state of _____.
Please provide the D/B/A (doing business as) number and commodity of public record that your company is authorized to collect debts and garnish wages.
Please evidence proof of the alleged debt including specifically the alleged contract or other instrument bearing my signature or application for services with my signature.

You should be aware that sending unsubstantiated demands for payment through the U.S. mail system might constitute mail fraud under federal law. Your failure to satisfy my request within the requirements of the Fair Debt Collections Act will be construed as your absolute waiver of any and all claims against me, and your tacit agreement to compensate me for costs and attorney fees.

> Thank You,
> Robert Boyd
> Social Security Number: 435-16-0719

Robert Boyd

Sample Letter Credit Bureau Dispute{ XE "Credit Bureau Dispute"

} and to prompt investigation

Robert Boyd
222 South Dixie Highway
Cave City, KY 42127

Certified mail number: _____

November 6, 2014

Disputed Account information :
(include creditors, addresses, and the account numbers)
Richland Credit Services   Account number #12345678
8732 Peachtree Street
Atlanta Georgia 30324
Date: 2-18-2012

Tribble & Boyd Collection services   Account number #876899877
4365 Connecticut Avenue
Dallas, Texas 34567
Date: 2-28-13

This letter is a formal complaint that you are reporting inaccurate and incomplete credit information on my credit report{ XE "credit report" }.

I am requesting validation of this debt based on the original credit application with my signature pursuant to 15 U.S.C. 1692(e), 15 U.S.C. 1692(g)(4) and Title 15 1666.

I understand that mistakes happen but your inaccurate information could cost me in higher interest rates for unsecured loans.

Can you please investigate the following information and either remove it or at the least send me the information that you used to add this item to my report.

Thank You,
Robert Boyd
Social Security Number: 435-16-0719

Robert Boyd

Dispute Letter Request to Describe Investigation Procedures

Robert Boyd
222 South Dixie Highway
Cave City, Kentucky 42127

Certified mail number: _____

November 6, 2014

[Name & address of Credit Bureau]
Equifax
P.O. Box 740123
Atlanta, Georgia 30374-0123

Re: Account number #1234221235

Dear Equifax:

This letter is a formal request for the description of the procedures used to determine the accuracy and completeness of the disputed information, including the business name, address, and telephone number of any furnisher{ XE "furnisher" } (credit or) of information contacted in connection with this re-investigation.

I am disappointed that you have failed to maintain reasonable procedures to assure complete accuracy in the information you publish and insist you comply with the law by providing the requested information within 15 days allowed.

For your benefit, I will restate the relevant dispute{ XE "dispute" } (if you do not plan to hold them liable in civil court).

Name of creditor or creditor(s), or debt collectors and Account number# 1234221235. As I have already stated, the listed item is inaccurate and incomplete and is a very serious error in your reporting. Please supply a corrected credit profile to all creditors who have received a copy within the last 6 months or the last one years for employment purposes.

Thank You,
Robert Boyd
Social Security number 435-16-0719

Robert Boyd

<u>Dispute Letter Sample 2 Credit Bureau</u>

Robert Boyd
222 South Dixie Highway
Cave City, Kentucky 42127

Certified mail number: _____

November 6, 2014

[Name & address of Creditor]
Equifax
P.O. Box 740123
Atlanta, Georgia 30374-0123

      RE: Dispute Letter
      Account number: #223213232

Dear Equifax:

This letter is a formal complaint that you are reporting inaccurate and incomplete credit information. As noticed: Your company has failed, to maintain reasonable procedures in your operations department to assure accuracy in the accounts.

The following information therefore needs to be investigated. Credit reporting laws ensure Bureaus report only 100 percent accurate information. I request to be provided proof of the alleged item, specifically the contract, note or other instrument bearing my signature. If this technique cannot be met, the item must be deleted from the report as soon as possible.

[Name of Creditor or Debt collector and account number]

Richland Credit Services   Account number #12345678

56

8732 Peachtree Street
Atlanta Georgia 30324
Date: 2-18-2012

Under federal law you have 30 days to complete your re-investigation. Please be advised that the description of the procedures used to determine the accuracy and completeness of the information is hereby requested as well, be provided within 15 days of the completion of your re-investigation or your firm is subject to civil liability based on the FCRA.

Thank You,
Robert Boyd
Social Security Number: 435-16-0719

Robert Boyd

<u>Dispute Letter Complaint with the Federal Trade Commission</u>

Robert Boyd
222 South Dixie Highway
Cave City, Kentucky 42127

Certified mail number: _____

November 6, 2014

FTC- Federal Trade Commission
Washington D.C. 20580
Phone: 1-877-382-4357

Re: Creditor non-response to dispute{ XE "dispute" } letters

I am writing to you based on the non response of several creditors that have not answered letters of dispute{ XE "dispute" } based on items and inquiries showing unpaid balances that are affecting my credit score and my credit history attached to the complaint are copies of certified mail slips as well as copies of the dispute letters and the dates of such. The companies listed failed to comply reasonable investigation methods and failed to produce documentation required by 15 U.S.C. Section 1666 proving indebtedness and validation of the debt pursuant to 1962(g)(4). Please investigate these companies and my complaint. Your work is greatly appreciated.

Attachments: DMV Collections
111 Bardstown Road
Louisville, Kentucky 42136
Account number: 785648290
Date: 3-25-2014
Most Hated Records, Films, and debt collections
213 Mammoth Cave Road
Lexington, Kentucky 40752

Thank You,
Robert Boyd
Social Security Number: 435-16-0719

58

CHAPTER 7: Unauthorized Credit Inquiry

NOW that you have learned about disputing the debt items on your credit report{ XE "credit report" }, it's time that you learn what a credit inquiry is. A credit inquiry which you will find at the end of your report see example 10. It is when a creditor or lender makes a pull into your credit report for the purposes of examining your credit history. As we have discussed beforehand. There are authorized inquires into your report or pulls that on a personal note are authorized pursuant to the FCRA.

For example, if you have applied for credit, insurance, rental, homeownership, or a job than these companies are authorized to make credit pulls which are called permissible pulls and you cannot do anything about those because you authorized them. Whenever you find that there was a pull on your credit report{ XE "credit report" } that was not authorized which is a non-permissible pull than you may hold that company liable if you did not apply for a job, credit, insurance, home ownership or rental Services with that company. Under the FCRA a company must have written instructions from the consumer (which is you) to whom the report relates in connection with a credit or job transaction including insurance and services. In accordance with the FCRA there is a statutory damages suit that you may also bring forth in federal court for settlements of 1,000 dollars and additional costs and attorney fees.

Before filing suit, you must send a letter see sample which is a notice that you are taking action against the company that made the unauthorized credit pull{ XE "unauthorized credit pull" }.

You must complete the letter with an extended offer to settle the unauthorized credit pull{ XE "unauthorized credit pull" } without litigation pursuant to Rule 68. Rule 68 prompts parties to a suit to evaluate the risks and costs of litigation and to balance them against the likelihood of success upon trial on the merits. Rule 68 allows a defendant to make a firm, non-negotiable offer of judgment and plaintiff may accept or refuse them.

Normally, as you can see in the sample letter, it is better to request for a Rule 68 offer of judgment{ XE "Rule 68 offer of judgment" } without attorney fees for a fast and speedy settlement.

Sometimes companies make unauthorized pulls of your credit so that may offer you a credit card or purchase a debt that you may have with another company. These unauthorized pulls are not qualified as permissible pulls and you may still take action in federal court.

Sometimes your credit report{ XE "credit report" } may have more than 20 non-permissible pulls onto your credit report. That's at least $20,000 dollars for you in statutory damages and $3,500 in Pro .Se legal fees times 20 which is $70,000 dollars for a total of $90,000. So without knowing, you could be sitting on a gold mind and all you need to do is fill out an application and apply for a credit report. Going Pro Se means that you are doing all the work without an attorney and District Courts are required to construe your claims liberally meaning, the court must interpret what you are saying-advocating expansive freedoms in accordance with Black's Law Dictionary ninth edition. Note: Once you have sent a letter to the company that has made the permissible pull. Don't forget to file your complaint with the Federal Trade Commission and credit bureau before filing suit in Federal Court and please keep all copies of letters sent including the copy of the certified mail slip. You will need this as evidence for your claim or suit in federal court as well as with the credit bureau.

In the sample I have provided on the next page is a sample motion for you to file your claim. Remember to sign all documents and provide the forma Pauperis affidavit. Remember there is a $350.00 court filing fee and the filing fee may be waived if you can prove that you have no supplemental income, meaning after your bills are paid, you don't have any extra cash or your extra cash is very minimal. In your Forma pauperis don't forget to include grocery expenses, gas, and daycare expenses and make sure to tap transactions of cost on file if needed which in most cases they are not. Good luck and remember to research case law pertaining to your unauthorized credit pull{ XE "unauthorized credit pull" } claim. If you do most of the work, you may find an attorney that will reimburse your Pro Se attorney fees after he wins your settlement if you hire him or her or a firm to help you litigate your case. Luckily I will provide you with sufficient responses that will aid you when these companies rebut your claims or fail to offer you a Rule 68 offer of judgment{ XE "Rule 68 offer of judgment" }. First is the actual sample of the suit and the forma pauperis in which you will file unless you plan to send the court the 350 dollar filing fee.

Dispute Letter Sample 41 To remove inquiry

Robert Boyd
222 South Dixie Highway
Cave City, Kentucky 42127

November 6, 2014

Most hated Records, films, & Debt Collections [Creditor or Debt Collector name:]
213 Mammoth Cave Road
Lexington, Kentucky 40752

RE: Unauthorized Credit Inquiry

To Whom It May Concern:

According to my most recent credit report{ XE "credit report" },
your company is currently reporting to the Big Three Credit Bureaus
that I applied for credit with your company or organization. I did not
grant you authorization to review my credit report.

The Fair Credit Reporting Act requires that a creditor be able to verify
the written authorization of the consumer giving the creditor
permission to review their credit. If you can provide a copy of a credit
application authorizing the disclosure of my credit files with my
signature, I will accept the inquiry. If a signed authorization cannot be
found, please remove the inquiry form the three main credit bureaus.

This inquiry is adversely affecting my credit report{ XE "credit
report" } and is impeding my ability to obtain necessary credit. Time
is of essence so I would greatly appreciate a response from you within
30 days or I will file a complaint with the Federal Trade Commission.
Please mail me the copy of the signed application or a letter indicating
your intention to delete this inquiry or I will have to take civil action in
federal court.

Thank you,
Robert Boyd
Social Security Number: 435-16-0719

Robert Boyd

Notice of Pending Litigation for Unauthorized Inquiry

Certified mail number: _____

Date: _____

Consumer/Plaintiff: (Your name)
(Your address)

To Defendant: (name of company that made the inquiry)
(Address)

RE: unauthorized credit inquiry

According to my most recent report, an inquiry (name of creditor) showed a non-permissible purpose pull that plaintiff did not authorize. Offering an opportunity to amicably settle violations to the FGRA-Fair Credit Reporting Act. Note: To constitute a permissible purpose pull a company or corporation must have written instructions from the consigner to whom the report relates in connection with a credit or job transaction.

Reasons for purpose pulls as affirmed by the FCRA are as follows (1) Plaintiff applied for credit, (2) Plaintiff applied for services (3) Plaintiff applied for employment. (4) Plaintiff applied for insurance. Plaintiff asserts under penalty of perjury that he has made no attempts to apply for credit, services, employment or insurance with

Pursuant to Rule 68, see Merek v Chesney 473 U.S. 1, 7 (1985). Rule

68 prompts parties to a suit to evaluate the risks and costs of litigation and to balance them against the likelihood of success upon trial on the merits. Rule 68 allows a defendant to make a firm, non-negotiable offer of judgment and plaintiff may accept or refuse them.

Plaintiff requests a settlement of 1,000.00 without statutory damages and costs without attorney fees or Plaintiff will proceed to federal court where jurisdiction is conferred by 15 U.S.C. § 1681p. and venue is proper pursuant to 28 U.S.C. § 1391b.

In the alternative, plaintiff in federal court will seek costs and attorney fees.

Robert Boyd

CHAPTER 8: Filing Your Civil Suit in Federal Court, Pro se

Filing your FCRA and FDCPA Claims in United States Federal Court Section 15 U.S.C. § S-2 (b) regulates that a furnisher{ XE "furnisher" } which is a lender or debt collector conduct an investigation with respect to the disputed information and to produce all documents showing indebtedness based on Title 15 Section 1666.

The FCRA imposes two sets of duties on furnishers as stated before,

1. To report the results of the investigation to the Credit Reporting Agency (Big 3); and
2. It prohibits any person or company from furnishing information to a credit reporting agency that the lender, debt collector, company, or person knows is inaccurate pursuant to Title 15 section 1666.

Section 1692 (e) l2 prohibits false representations or deceptive means to collect a debt see sample that cannot be legally taken. If a debt collector blocks his or her calls after you have requested them to stop calling based in part that they have not proven indebtedness. They may be held liable pursuant to the FDCPA for statutory damages of $1,000 per phone call. See also sample that stops total collection practices based on attempts to collect debt(s) without showing your indebtedness. The federal suit must be filed in the District Court of your residence. See sample for District Courts in your state or circuit. The sample is an exhibit of an FCRA lawsuit or complaint. At the top of the claim place the name of the District Court from which State or circuit you will be filing from and to based on your residence. For example, the 6th circuit includes the States of Kentucky, Ohio, Tennessee and Michigan. So if you are filing a lawsuit and your residence is located in Louisville, Kentucky then your suit would be filed in the United States District Court for the Western District of Kentucky see circuit court example. The plaintiff is you and there is no case number yet so place NA or Not applicable in that space. The defendant is the lender, debt collector, or Credit Bureau whom you are filing suit against. The preliminary statement is the action for damages in which you are bringing against the company whom you are suing or litigating against. Jurisdiction is conferred by 15 U.S.C. §1681p which is the statue stating that the District Court has jurisdiction to hear your claim. Venue is conferred by 28 U.S.C. § 1391b which is subject to the same requirements as jurisdiction which is based on the circuit court in which you are filing. The next section is the factual allegations section which provides you with the opportunity to provide the court with all exhibits such as copies of all letters and certified mail slips sent to the lender or debt collector see sample page 2. The next section is the list of counts that you are suing or: litigating for. When a lender or debt collector places a debt for collection without showing indebtedness pursuant to Title 15 section 1666, the lender has violated 15 U.S.C. § 1692e (2) by falsely representing the amount, character, amount, or legal status of the debt. If the Company or lender made phone calls than the standard section would be 1692d which prohibits a debt collector from engaging in any conduct of which is to harass, oppress, or abuse any person in connection with the collection of debt. 1692F arises when a debt collector abuses its superior economic position and level of sophistication which is always a code section violation when bringing suit against a debt collector. Even if the phone calls are not answered by plaintiff.

A claim pursuant to Title 15 U.S.C. § 1692 (5) claim has arisen see Big Apple BMW 974 F.2d at 1563 and Rush v Portfolio Recovery Association 2013 U.S. Dist Lexis 149288 (2013).

Name the creditor as a debt collector and reference it to title code 15 section 1666 and 1692(e). Than file a dispute{ XE "dispute" } to the Federal Trade commission see sample Please mail all certified mail receipts and copies of letters or dispute letters that you mailed to the lenders or debt collectors so that you can support your claim, (Do not send originals and always sign your name in red ink so that when the paper is copied the red ink cannot be dilated or changed like common colors of blue and black which can be remade). Note that debt collectors are also bound by title code section 15 -1666 and cannot take action on claims that cannot be legally taken if these lenders or debt collectors cannot prove indebtedness. Remember to also send a letter to the Credit Bureau to give them notice that the item is in dispute. This letter is needed before litigation (lawsuit) in federal court can take place.

In the United States District Court For
[where the District of Court is see example]
Example -The Western District Of Kentucky

Plaintiff
[You are the plaintiff in civil action against another]
Robert Boyd

VS

Case Number: [if a case number place here
but you don't have one yet but once in court you
will have a case number]

Defendant
[The company you are suing]
Example: Tribble Collection Services

Civil Complaint{ XE "Civil Complaint" }

NOW COMES [Plaintiff/your name] appearing through Pro Se counsel and
hereby moves this court to bring an action for damages brought for
violations of the FCRA, Fair Credit Reporting Act 15 U.S.C. § 1681
and Plaintiff requests to move in Forma Pauperis{ XE "Forma
Pauperis" }.

Jurisdiction and Venue

1. Jurisdiction of this court if conferred by Title 1.5 U.S.C.
   Section §1681p
2. Venue is proper in this circuit pursuant to 28 U.S.C. 1391b

All conditions precedent to the bringing of this action have been
performed, waived, or excused.

Factual Allegations

1. The conditions to obtain permissible purpose to make a pull of
   Plaintiff's consumer report as per FCRA 15 U.S.C. § 1681b are
   not being met by defendant.

71

2. Since (date of noticed unauthorized inquiry) Plaintiff's Experian consumer report keeps showing a non-permissible pull that the plaintiff is not authorizing and have been made by defendant see exhibit A. (Exhibit A. should be a copy of your credit report{ XE "credit report" } where the unauthorized inquiry or pull was first identified.)

3. On (date of letter sent to the company who made the pull) an unauthorized credit inquiry or pull was sent via certified mail number (certified mail slip number) requesting to have the inquiry removed and for a rule 68 offer of judgment and to Send proof of permissible purpose of this pull to plaintiff.

4. Plaintiff respectfully comes, and ask, and demands to this court, remedy to all FCRA violations against plaintiff and committed by defendant.

Count 1

Violation of Fair Credit Reporting Act pursuant to 15 U.S.C. § 1681 and willful non compliance by defendant

1. Paragraphs 1 through 6 are re-alleged as though fully set forth herein.

2. The definition of a consumer within the meaning of FCRA § 1681a (c) describes the plaintiff.

3. The definition of a corporation within the meaning of FCRA 15 U.S.C. § 1681a (b) describes the defendant.

4. The conditions to obtain permissible purpose to make a pull of plaintiff's consumer report pursuant to FCRA 15 U.S.C. § 1681b are not being met by defendant.

Plaintiff's Experian Report (name all reports containing unauthorized pull) keeps showing non-permissible inquiries/pulls that plaintiff is not authorizing that are being made by defendant.

Wherefore plaintiff demands judgment for damages in the amount of 1,000 dollars and for actual damages and also requests attorney fees, costs under a Pro Se financial hardship ability in preparing documents under the standard paralegal fee doctrine of this state pursuant to FCRA 15 U.S.C. § 1681n (a) (3) and 15 U.S.C. § 16810(a) against defendant.

Conclusion

Plaintiff hereby demands a trial by jury of all issues so triable as a matter of law.

Dated: [date of motion]　　　　　　　　　Respectfully Submitted,
　　　　　　　　　　　　　　　　　　　　[Your name typed here]

_____
Signature
[Your address]
[City, State Zip]

Certificate of Service

I, [Your name] _____ do swear under penalty of perjury 28 U.S.C.§1746 that the following motion is a verified true and correct declaration of events and was mailed to the District Court via United States pre-paid mail on this _____ day of _____, 2014. [date]

[name of Court and Address here]
The Western District Of Kentucky
Street Address
City, State Zip

_____
Signature

Robert Boyd

In the United States District Court For
[where the District of Court is see example]
Example -The Western District Of Kentucky

Plaintiff
[You are the plaintiff in civil action against another]
Robert Boyd

VS	Case Number: [if a case number place here but you don't have one yet but once in court you will have a case number]

Defendant
[The company you are suing]
Example: Tribble Collection Services

Civil Complaint{ XE "Civil Complaint" }

NOW COMES (your name) appearing through Pro Se counsel and hereby moves this court to bring an action for damages brought for violations of the FCRA, Fair Debt Collection Practices Act{ XE "Fair Debt Collection Practices Act" } 15 U.S.C. § 1692 and Plaintiff requests to move in Forma Pauperis{ XE "Forma Pauperis" }.

Jurisdiction and Venue

1. Jurisdiction of this court is conferred by Title 15 U.S.C. Section §1681p
2. Venue is proper in the circuit pursuant to 28 U.S.C. §1391b

All conditions precedent to the bringing of this action have been performed, waived, or excused.

Factual Allegations

3. Defendant violated the FDCPA by falsely representing the character, amount, or legal status of a debt, based on 15 U.S.C. 1692(e) and 15 U.S.C. 1692(e)(2).

4. Since (date of noticed and alleged debt found on your credit report{ XE "credit report" }) Plaintiff's Equifax consumer report (include Experian and Transunion if they apply) keeps showing a debt owed for collection (or just owed debt if a credit lender), and defendant has failed to evidence the owed debt pursuant to title 15 Section 1666 and 15 U.S.C. 1692(g)(4) upon request for to show Plaintiff's indebtedness.

5. On (date of letter sent to the company, debt collector, or lender) a notice for validation of debt and to cease and desist collection activities per dispute{ XE "dispute" } of alleged debt was mailed to (defendant) (include copy of letter sent with certified mail slip number)

6. Plaintiff respectfully comes, and asks, and demands to this court, remedy to all FDCPA violations against Plaintiff and committed by defendant.

Count 1

7. Paragraphs 1-6 are re-alleged as though fully set herein.

8. The definition of a consumer within the meaning of FDCPA 15 U.S.C. 1692a (3) describes the plaintiff.

9. The definition of a debt collector within the meaning of FDCPA 15 U.S.C. §1692a (6) describes the defendant.

10. Defendant violated the FDCPA. Defendant violations include,but are not limited to the following.

    A. Defendant violated 15 U.S.C. 1692(e) and 1692e(2) by falsely representing the character, amount, or legal status of any debt.

    B. Defendant violated 15 U.S.C. § 1692e(10) by the use of any false representation or deceptive means to collect or attempt to collect any debt or to obtain information concerning a consumer.

    C. Defendant violated 15 U.S.C. §1692f by the use of unfair and unconscionable means to collect the alleged debt.

Wherefore, Plaintiff demands judgment for damages against defendant, and 1,000 for actual or statutory damages, punitive damages, attorney fees, and costs pursuant to FGRA 15 U.S.C. §1681n(a)(3),FCPA 15 U.S.C. §1681o(a) and FDCPA 15 U.S.C. §1692k.

Conclusion

Plaintiff demands for a jury trial pursuant to Amendment 7 of the constitution.

Dated: [date of motion]

Respectfully Submitted,
[Your name typed here]

_____
Signature
[Your address]
[City, State Zip]

Certificate of Service

I, [Your name] _____ do swear under penalty of perjury 28 U.S.C.§1746 that the following motion is a verified true and correct declaration of events and was mailed to the District Court via United States pre-paid mail on this _____ day of _____, 2014. [date]

[name of Court and Address here]
The Western District Of Kentucky
Street Address
City, State Zip

_____
Signature

Robert Boyd

In the United States District Court For
[where the District of Court is see example]
Example -The Western District Of Kentucky

Plaintiff
[You are the plaintiff in civil action against another]
Robert Boyd

VS	Case Number: [if a case number place here but you don't have one yet but once in court you will have a case number]

Defendant
[The company you are suing]
Example: Tribble Collection Services

AFFIDAVIT IN SUPPORT
OF REQUEST TO PROCEED IN FORMA PAUPERIS

I, _____, declare that I am the plaintiff petitioner in the above captioned proceeding; that in support of my motion to proceed without being required to prepay fees or costs or give security therefore, I state that because of my poverty. I am unable to pay the costs of said proceeding or to give security therefore; and, that I believe that I am entitled to redress.

I further declare that the responses which I make to the questions and instructions below are true.

1. Are you presently employed? ☐ Yes ☐ No

   A. If the answer is yes, state the amount of your salary or

wages per month and give the name and address of your employer. _____

    B. If the answer is no, state the date of you last worked and the amount of salary or wages per month which you received.

_____

2. Have you received within the past TWELVE (12) MONTHS any money from any of the following sources?

    A. Business, profession, or form of self-employment?
        ☐ Yes ☐ No

    B. Pensions, annuities, or life insurance payments?
        ☐ Yes ☐ No

    C. Rent payments, interest, or dividends? ☐ Yes ☐ No
    D. Gifts or inheritances?   ☐ Yes ☐ No
    E. Any other resources?   ☐ Yes ☐ No

If the answer to any of the above is yes, describe each source of money received and state the amount received from each during the past TWELVE (12) MONTHS.

_____

_____

_____

4. Do you have any cash, or do you have money in a checking or savings account?

☐ Yes ☐ No

If yes, how much do you have? $_____

5. Do you own any real estate (house and/or property), stocks, bonds, notes, automobiles, or other valuable property, excluding ordinary household goods and furnishings?

□ Yes □ No

A. If the answer is yes, describe the property and state its approximate value.

_____

_____

B. If the answer is yes, list any mortgages, liens, or loans against the property and state the amount you owe.

_____

_____

6. List the persons who are dependent upon you for their support. State your relationship to those persons and indicate how much you contribute toward their support.

_____

_____

_____

Signed this _____ day of _____, 2014.

Plaintiff/Petitioner

_____

Signature of Plaintiff/Petitioner

DECLARATION UNDER PENALTY OF PERJURY

YOU MUST DECLARE UNDER PENALTY OF PERJURY THAT THE ANSWERS YOU HAVE GIVEN HEREIN ARE TRUE AND CORRECT. GIVING A FALSE ANSWER OR FALSE INFORMATION IN RESPONSE TO ANY QUESTION WILL SUBJECT YOU TO FEDERAL PERJURY CHARGES. 18 U.S.C. §1621 PROVIDES AS FOLLOWS:

Whoever —

......

(2) in any declaration, certificate, verification, or Statement under penalty of perjury as permitted under section 1746 of title 28, United States Code, willfully subscribes as true any material matter which he does not believe to be true;

is guilty of perjury and shall, except as otherwise expressly provided by law, be fined not more than $2,000 or imprisoned not more than five years, or both. This section is applicable whether the statement or subscription is made within or without the United States.

Understanding the above, I declare under penalty of perjury that the foregoing answers and information provided by me in support of my request to proceed in forma pauperis are true and correct.

Executed this _____ day of _____, 2014.

_____
Signature of Plaintiff/Petitioner

This must be attached to your claim.

CHAPTER 9: Keeping Good Credit

Once you have cleared your credit report{ XE "credit report" } by disputing the debts and have raised your score slightly to a modest range. Now is the time to begin to build your credit, (Note that at any time you can piggyback someone else's score for fees roughly between $500 to $1,000 depending on your broker or Debt Consolidator. (Piggybacking is the concept of using someone else's score or credit who has a high score for a number of years and for that time period your score will be the same as theirs.) One way to build your Credit is to walk in a Rent-A-Center or Rentway store and fill out an application to finance something that is less expensive and easy to pay off. Example: The Kindle Fire is being sold for a whopping $199.00 without tax included. Financing through Rentway or Rent-a-center at a high interest rate over the next 2 years will probably be a weekly payment of 5 dollars per week. Doesn't sound like much huh but if you do the arithmetic (math) then you're actually paying $480 dollars for a two hundred dollar Kindle that would have only cost $200 plus in cold hard cash. The main reason is because interest rates for financed items at these types of stores compound bi-weekly or monthly and when you pay the minimum than your only paying on the interest but that is another story that we will not discuss in this book. Back to the concept. Now let's say that at the time of your financing of the Kindle, your checking account contained $700 dollars in cash and $2,000 in savings. Now, it is without a doubt that you can pay for the Kindle with cash but as of now, you are establishing credit and you want to establish your credit fast. By placing a $40 dollar down payment which is double the standard 10 percent for non home purchases, you have established a willingness to pay off your purchases. For the next few weeks, every time that you make the $5 payment. Pay an extra ten dollars on the principle of the account. Paying on the principle means that you're making a payment on the actual balance and not the interest rate. Now after about three months of paying on the bill, take the $200 that you were going to pay for the kindle Fire and pay off the bill, which will probably be around $110 to $130 dollars depending on the compounded interest. Yes, you may have paid an extra $40 for the kindle but you established a credit history for timely payments and for paying off debts at a prolific rate, (faster than normal).

Now that you have established good credit, it's time to take a trip to the car dealership and finance the car of your dreams. Maybe it's a Camaro, maybe a Cadillac or maybe it's the Boyd Signature Series 900 but wait! Going to the dealership could mean more debt, but hey, you earned it, right? You invested in a book on how to restore your credit, disputed the debts, and now your claims are being argued in court for a small settlement instead of wasting your money on beer and hotdogs to watch the game with your buddies or for a French manicure (for the ladies who purchase this book). And who wouldn't want to drive the car of their dreams while being instagrammed with the top down smiling on Facebook.

Everyone will want to hang out with you and your significant other will be falling head over heels. But hold up just a second and allow me to give you the tips of your life or in Other words "GAME". After paying off that Kindle your feeling your worth. Now it's time to go to the bank for a personal loan. Let's say the new PlayStation 4 is now on sale. Even though you have established a good foundation by paying off the Kindle. The bank tells you that the $500 dollar personal loan will need to be secured by a secured loan. A secured loan, is a loan where your money is placed inside the bank with a lien on it, basically being collateral against the personal loan. Once the monies are returned and the personal loan is paid in full. Your secured money will be released back into your account. Now the average person thinks, hey why would I finance a Playstation® 4 and end up paying $550 or $600 when I can purchase it for $400 dollars in cold hard cash. Easy question, saving small amounts of cash will not lead you to financial stability. But establishing a credit history backed by timely payments will help you build an elusive credit line for mass purchases. Just follow me to this road to financial freedom. Now you're at the bank and you have agreed to the $500 dollar personal loan for a secured loan against $600 of your own personal dollars. The bank agrees to loan you this $500 dollars for a period of 18 months for low monthly payments of $40 dollars per month. Costing you $720 dollars for $ 400 dollar Playstation® 4.

Of course 18 months is a long time to wait on the hot rod of your dreams but keep in mind, you have better plans with the banks money than the bank has ever imagined.

Although Bill Gates and Donald Trump are billionaires, most of their financing does not come from their personal bank accounts. It comes from banks and other lenders who take risks for minimal gains that can equal millions of dollars. But hey, you're no way near a billion dollars but you are on the right path to financial freedom. So imagine that you sign the agreement for the personal loan and you begin to make payments for a couple of months.

Keep in mind not to spend the $400 dollars that you had set to the side because in another month, your plans are to pay off the remaining balance of the personal loan. Now let's say, that the company you are working for allows you to get a little overtime, on a Saturday afternoon which normally pays time in a half. For example, when I was young and attending college I worked as a die cast operator for JL French Die Cast. One of the largest die cast plants in the United States for 15.60 per hour. So on a Saturday afternoon I would earn about $22.90 per hour for an 8 hour work day which after taxes would normally equal to a hundred extra dollars on my check at the end of the week. The most common mistake that everyday working class people make is the thought that they deserve a new pair of shoes or a night out under the city lights with the extra monies earned. But that is the way a consumer thinks and there is a difference in a consumer - a person who works to make purchases and a consumer opportunist{ XE "opportunist" } - a person who works but manages his or her funds versus economic change. Meaning that money is not made to spend on things that will depreciate tomorrow, though the Playstation® 4 will depreciate in time. It's really an asset because Playstation® only débuts new game consoles every 5 to 7 years and for that time period, your Playstation® 4 will still hold its value at the pawn shop or yard sale if needed and your only plan is to create a credit history of timely payments. So instead of making another purchase, the best thing to do is to take the extra one hundred dollars and pay 50 dollars on the principle of the personal loan, place 20 more dollars in your checking, and blow the rest on a movie with your significant other. Now that you have paid on the Playstation® 4 for nearly three months by paying the monthly $40 per month payments and placing at least $20 per month on the principle of the account. It's time to take that initial $400 that you had kept in your checking account and pay off the loan in one lump sum. It will probably seem like credit card applications are flooding your mail box and now the bank wants to loan you more money because your credit score within one year of obtaining your credit report{ XE "credit report" } has elevated to a 700. Now it's ok to at least fill out the credit application and receive the credit cards as long as the cards are unsecured (meaning it will not cost you a lien against, your own money to receive the credit card) but make sure there are no annual fees or at least the annual fees are not expensive but remember. There is still no time for a spending frenzy. Unsecure credit cards are only for back up plans just in case your employer decides that your pension is not in the budget plans and your about to be layed off or just in case the government shuts down and your company is funded by the government and your working without a paycheck. So it's been only 5 months since you have established good credit and nearly 10 months since you have cleared your credit report and it hasn't cost you anything but a few extra hundred bucks that you paid for finance charges for a Kindle Fire and a Sony Playstation® 4, It hasn't been a year yet and you've secured yourself a promising future instead of filing bankruptcy or paying a debt consolidator monthly payments at a third of your debt owed for the next 3 to 5 years. Now it's time to take that trip to the dealership to purchase the car of your dreams and because you have established a repetitive history of timely payments, the car dealership tells you that you don't need a cosigner or a down payment. But wait, the $28,000 your about to pay for the new Camaro or Dodge Challenger with all options will cost you roughly $500 monthly not including insurance premiums at $250 monthly. That's about 40 percent of your monthly income and who knows if your employer won't fall victim to a slow economy and file for Chapter 11. Yes, I want you to own the car of your dreams but let's do what most people don't do as Albert Einstein once stated, "Think". So while you were searching the web or the local newspaper (preferably the Courier-Journal, Wall Street Journal, or the USA Today) and you noticed while you were searching for a nice used vehicle with low miles and driving the Camaro that the dealership gave to you for a week so that you would fall in love with it and if they've guessed it right, you've already told the girls around the city that the car is yours and now the girls are in love with the car more than you. So the average Joe, to avoid the embarrassment and to be cool and fill deserving of the purchase will take on this financial hardship of 5 to 6 years of car payments without even thinking of other possibilities and why not. Doesn't Jay-Z and Sean "Puffy" Combs ride around in Bentleys all day while calling shots in the entertainment industry. Sure they do, but they do it at the expense of others, this is the difference of being a consumer (the poor and middle class who work to pay for the fads of the world) and entrepreneurs (the rich) who take the money they earn and invest the money into businesses that earn them money to pay for their fads of the world, see the difference. Remember the Dodge Magnum, it was a cool car, with a lot of features but it was discontinued shortly and the people who broke their neck to finance the car.

Are just now paying off the bill and guess what, nobody drives dodge magnums anymore. Dodge has suspended the line and now that $33,000 dollar car that cost you $40,000 after 6 to 7 years of payments is worthless because it's no longer in style and do you know what's worse. The car dealerships won't even give you a $5,000 dollar trade in value on the vehicle for a trade in for a newer car. Let's say you're looking into the classified section and you see a large advertisement that reads:

"PUBLIC AUTO AUCTION"
Tuesday night at 7 p.m.

The best thing about auctions are that if you have cash or a floating loan{ XE "floating loan" } with the bank. You can purchase vehicles for a fraction maybe a fourth of the price that you would normally pay at the car lot. At the public auction a fee is normally required of $300 dollars if you plan to make a purchase which will be returned at the end of the night if you choose not to purchase a vehicle and if you do. The $300 will go toward the purchase of the vehicle. (Note there is also a $25 non-refundable fee if you want to sell your own vehicle at the auction). Since you've probably never been to a Public Auto Auction, I'll tell you how it works. Some cars are run through the auction by car dealers, car dealerships, or individual people. The cars are usually trade-ins and most of than have some sort of problem such as a broken tail light, water pump, or a transmission problem, etc. The damages will vary per automobile. The exception and advantage is that before the auction and any time during the auction, you as a potential buyer will be allowed to take a mechanic with you to the parking lot where the cars are parked so that he can instruct you on what is wrong with the vehicle and estimate the cost of the damages. During the auction the dealer will start off at a high price but he will go down when no one bids on the vehicle depending on his investment which is most times minimal. Normally a vehicle, for example that will sell for around $7,000 for example a 2009 Dodge Charger but would have cost you $22,000 brand new. Would sell for $1,500 to $3,000 dollars at the auction. So let's say the Camaro cost around $30,000 brand new. Then at the auction with a few thousand miles it may cost you around $12,000, which is around $18,000 in savings for the same vehicle except there is only a few thousand extra miles on it but it still saves you a pretty penny. But who has $12,000 in cash just lying around for a rainy day. This is where good credit factors in. Since the only difference in the 2013 Camaro and the 2010 Camaro is the dashboard besides a couple minor options, why not take advantage of the 2010 which will probably cost you less than $12,000 at the auction, I'd say around $5,500. Not only are you saving but imagine what you can do with the extra cash that you would be spending in monthly payments for the new Camaro. Now it's time to give the bank a call or it's time for a meeting at the bank with the loan department so that you can explain to them the scenario of the auction and they inform you that they will agree to finance a vehicle for you with less than 100,000 miles as long as the vehicle is no more than 5 years old. The bank also agrees to a floating loan to cover any check that you write for vehicle purchases of up to $12,000 for used vehicle or $30,000 for a new vehicle. This is the best news you have heard all year long. So for the next few weeks you visit the auction and there are no Camaros up for bid but the next week you find one and win the bid at around $5,200 and you write the check for the amount of monies owed although you will need to wait until the next day for the check to clear. The only problem with the vehicle is a simple fuel pump which will cost you around $400 dollars in maintenance work but that's ok. You just saved a lot of money and you still have the car of your dreams at around $200 dollars per month for 36 months. Are you following me? I've purchased numerous cars at the auto auction in Glendale, Kentucky and I've bought 3 cars at times that on a car lot would have cost me the price of one of those cars.

Let's say, after 2 and a half years, you're getting restless at your job and you want to quit or find something more challenging and you have six months to pay off your Camaro which is still in style because for the next 3 years Chevrolet never changed the body style of your car so a person on the outside looking in cannot tell the difference between a 2017 and your 2010. Just like the BMW 325i from 1993 to 1998. Or the Grand Cherokee from 1993 to 1999. So let's say you've been saving $100 per month from your check deposits and half of your $2,000 dollar yearly tax return, so now you're looking at around $6,600 in savings plus the $1,500 you already had in savings, so you're holding on to around $8,100 in savings. You've gotten a bright idea lately, that you're tired of working for a firm or company that doesn't appreciate your work or you're ready for growth and the company you work for is not allowing you a chance to move up through the ranks. So you do the research on small businesses and through entrepreneur magazine etc. and Black Enterprise and you learn that an 18 wheeler cost around $100,000 dollars but for $25,000 you can purchase a used one which may make you a ton of money for the next couple of years.

Instead of vacationing this year on your weekly vacation, you decide to attend a one week CDL Class because you've just learned that truck drivers earn $1.40 per mile for owner operators which after gas, necessities, and insurance leaves you with about $2,000 dollars per week if you're running 3,500 miles after expenses. Normally a one to two week CDL training course will cost you $6,000 in financing but it's only a fourth of the cost if you're paying cash so you invest $2,000 from your savings toward this CDL training which leaves you with around $6,000 in cash. After forming an LLC the bank agrees to loan you up to $40,000 for a truck with new tires, and other necessities needed for a truck with less than 600,000 miles on it. So you find a truck for $23,000 and after expenses you're looking at around $31,000 but you decide to borrow the whole $40,000 so that you will have room for error and you place the $2,000 that you paid for the school with, back into your account and your payment is roughly $700 monthly for the next 6 years. So you start earning around $1,800 per week after gas expenses of about $2,200 a week because you have quit your other job and now you work for yourself driving around 3,500 miles per week and your savings $200 per week in your 401K, $200 per week in your savings, $300 per week for your maintenance repairs and the rest you spend on bills, wants, and needs. And yes, Louboutins, Air Max, and Michael Jordan's are cool to own. Just don't get excessive with buying different colors.

Air Jordan's are wants not needs but that's ok. Because now, your money is working for you and your Camaro is paid off and now with the extra $900 per week after your savings, you can afford a new Camaro and of course. The Bank agrees to finance a brand new Camaro which doesn't even factor into the $7,200 your making per month now. So after a couple of years and you've saved up around $20,500 not counting your 401K savings or company maintenance repair savings and you add that to the $7,000 that you had in initial savings and you're looking at around $27,800 in savings. Your girlfriend wants to get married and start a family but hey, you don't own a house. She's tired of renting and really wants a house so you shop around for these expensive $150,000 to $250,000 dollar houses as well as a $5,000 dollar wedding ring. Something 5 years ago you couldn't even dream of doing. So let's say since the mortgage crisis, banks want 10 to 20 percent down payment before they ok a home loan and while you're searching for the home of your dreams.

You find a two story vinyl siding house for around $20,000 in a rough neighborhood that need minor repairs. Of course your fiancé will not agree on the purchase but you explain to her that the house has been appraised at $85,000 and you can see the advantages of using the two story home for rent to the public, so you go against your fiancé's wishes and purchase the house with cash for around $16,000. After minor repairs, you place a rent sign on the home and you rent out the down stairs as well as the upstairs to college kids or other people from that neighborhood at $350 dollars per month. The bank agrees to refinance the house or you may place a lien on the house for up to $70,000 so you place the $25,000 that you spent from your savings back into your account and now you're looking at $50,000 dollars toward the purchase of your dream home and end the payment is only $500 per month on the home so your clipping around $200 dollars per month in extra income from rent. Now you can purchase your fiancé the ring of her dreams and put at least $40,000 down on the home of your dreams while the renters are paying off your loan and you're living the American dream. Sounds like a plan huh. This is why good credit is important. So that no one can never tell you the one word that everyone hates, NO!.

Years ago a colleague of mine and myself started a local record company called Most Hated Records. We had $10,000 in actual funding and my colleague had a 700 credit score which allowed us to pay for flyers, CD press kits, and other materials needed with the cash while we financed the equipment instead of buying the equipment which would have left us with no monies for the additional tools we needed. We were able to convince Mr. Serv on, a gold selling artist on No limit records at the time to rap on a track for our upcoming CD for $1,500 dollars and Big V of the Platinum group the Nappy Roots also agreed to the same contract. We then used BCD Music group for distribution purposes and the album was nationwide and caught the attention of TVT Records home at the time to rap artists Yo Gotti and Cuban sensation Pit Bull.

The deal went sour and we placed another $50,000 into the studio but all of this could not have been done without good credit. The album was a local success but not a success for Soundscan due to promotional technicalities but it was a success as far as business strategy. Who would have ever thought that two locals could go nationwide without a record company backing them but we did just that while also filing taxes on the companies gains and losses for years. Now let's go back to the Bob Johnson's (former owner of B.E.T) and the Oprah Winfrey's, Tyler Perry's, Kevin Hart's, the Paul Allen's, and the Warren Buffet's of the world. These people form LLC's which are limited liability companies that protect their assets during litigation (lawsuits) and from Bankruptcy's. Master P who has a net worth of $350 million was able to file for bankruptcy for a studio that had cost him $60 million because the studio was no longer making money but his assets were protected against the loan because the studio was in the name of an LLC instead of his personal name. As you can see, good credit can serve the same purposes as cash and don't forget that good credit will allow the rental of that nice building for that after party after your wedding so that you can get back some of the monies you spent funding the wedding because before most people will rent to you. They want to know your credit score to ensure that they are dealing with good standing American citizens who will protect their assets. The time to clean your credit and head toward financial freedom is now so what are you waiting for.

Robert Boyd

CHAPTER 10: Maintaining & Balancing Your Credit

There are several ways to keep your credit rating at its highest peak. One way is to apply for a credit report{ XE "credit report" } every 12 months. Though you may have maintained an elusive credit history, people steal identities at a vast rate. People will use your identity to finance items and by receiving a credit report yearly, you can dispute{ XE "dispute" } these items as "not mines". You may also want to litigate those furnishers and debt collectors that have made unauthorized inquiries on your credit report. Another way is to pay your bills on time and whenever you get some extra cash. Take a percentage and pay on the principle of the account this way at least your paying on the actual amount of the loan and not the interest. Another way is to search for hidden and annual fees when applying for credit cards and try your best to receive fixed rate loans so that your payment is locked in and always the same. Keep credit card debt to a minimum because the fees and interest evolve 90 days and sometimes even monthly. The longer it takes for you to pay off a credit card, the more interest you'll be paying and you'll end up paying $300 dollars for a pair of Air Max or House of Dereon heels for your girlfriend that only cost $100 dollars. What about Bankruptcy Mr. Boyd? filing for bankruptcy could be an option of a business trying to stop the liquidation of its assets and to protect you against your creditors but not by disputing debts because if these companies cannot prove your indebtedness within the meaning of Title 15 section 1666 than you will not be entitled to pay them and the item must be removed from your credit report. Pursuant to Title 15 U.S.C. 1692(e) debt collectors cannot take action without a validation of the debt which is an agreement signed by you from the original creditor.

CHAPTER 11: Wants Over Needs Basically, Being a Consumer

Sometimes, everyday working class people tend to get confused about what products are wants which are liabilities and what are considered needs which are necessities. An example of a need is a pair of shoes. Most people place a heavy value on their feet and why not. It's the first place a woman looks at after she's noticed a man's face and it's also the second place a man's looks at after he notices the females body which is most times a more attractive trait than a females facial appearance. Men and women both are attentive to the shoes on the feet of the opposite sex. A person's shoes will tell you (1) If a person has on dirty shoes, you may think that they are an unclean person. (2) They may not care about their appearance or their job title requires them to get a little dirty. But clean shoes or heels on a woman can help you imagine the finances of the opposite sex or their financial class in some cases. Just because Lebron James or Kim Kardashian is rocking a new pair of shoes doesn't mean you have to purchase every single one of them that you see. Celebrities get paid millions of dollars to wear the shoes and clothes of big name designers and most of the time they only wear them during an event and never wear them again. It's the same for vehicles. Rapper and Mogul Baby owner of Cashmoney records once owned 50 expensive cars but he learned that if he saved the cash from purchasing those cars. He could use the cash to start other businesses and eventually he sold most of those vehicles and invested the monies into a publishing company which debuted his recent book titles on New York Times and was still able to maintain some of those vehicles while increasing his net worth. Just remember you can only drive one car at a time. It's good to have a van, a sport utility vehicle, one old classic, a motor bike, a car for your wife, maybe an everyday car like a Mercedes or dodge charger and a ford focus for back up. Anything after that is highly excessive and increases your chances of defaulting on payments, loans, and other agreements. In time, your wants will turn into liabilities when the cars won't start up in the morning and now your spending your capitol (cash) to get them repaired at the body shop or even worse. You don't have the capitol and you charge the repairs on your credit card and now you've acquired more debt. This method works the same for clothes, DVD's, and other material but by investing in land. You can always place a lien on the property or sell it later on for a higher value or just get your money back. If property isn't an option, try a certificate of Deposit at the bank (sometimes referred to as a CD) or even a junk bond. One of the best messages in today's generation was during a stand up hosting of the B.E.T. awards in which comedian Kevin Hart stated that most people had yes men but what people need are no men. People that will stop them from making excessive purchases and these no men protect people of the most dangerous people alive, "THEMSELVES". When you're choosing your teammates (friends, employer, Banks). Make sure these people are in your circle for a reason other than that you played sea saw together in first and second grade although loyalty is a great asset. Surround yourself with people who will help you determine the difference in needs such as soap, detergent, diapers, gas, oil, and want's, Both colors of the new Air Jordan's, a hard top and a drop top Bentley, and different color Louboutins. And if you're a professional ball player and you don't know what to do with your money, then just let it sit in the bank and draw interest and the most important thing to do. Finish your education and get up and learn a new trade. Whether it's securing your G.E.D., an associate degree, or a janitorial certificate it stabilizes your environment so you don't have to keep looking at the rear view. In the words of Russell Simmons, "you can stare through the windshield and see what's coming at you instead of worrying about what's behind you." This is the power of thinking, what Einstein was telling you about years before. Plan for the day but set goals for the future and stop putting things off. You can start your plan for a better financial future today.

Robert Boyd

CHAPTER 12: What Can Be Purchased With Good Credit?

Anything can be purchased with good credit. From jewelry, to land, vacant lots, clothes, books, businesses, and even a night on the town in Vegas with the lady of your dreams. Sometimes, employers seek your credit score before hiring you for a job and some employer's even want your credit score on your job application or your resume. Even Real Estate Agents and property rental agents want your credit score before they will give you a tour of a home for purchase or rent. Even 5 star restaurants in Hollywood want your credit score for your table reservation before they will even give you a table in their restaurant.

People frown upon bad credit in this country. Remember when the U.S. lost their Triple A credit rating. China stated that they no longer considered the U.S. the number one global economic power. Much of this was based on the decision making on what led them into losing their credit rate and the same works for you. A person with bad credit is not a good decision maker. When the credit rating was lowered to a double A credit score.

The price of crude oil cost companies such as Exxon more money and now the price of a gallon has soured to 3.85 in most states instead of the 1.95 it should be. Do you know that when the United States receives there Triple A rating again, the price to finance crude oil will lower but companies such as Exxon will not lower the price. They will keep making profits off the citizens of America while politicians get kickbacks for their campaigns from these types of large companies who will again cause a default just to lower the credit rating. This way, the rich get richer and the poor stay poor because your extra money is spent on gasoline so Exxon makes you pay a tariff{ XE "tariff" }- which is an increased tax on goods, for the oil while they play cat and mouse with the credit score to profit off your money. So why not stop being a consumer and start your way to financial freedom. Stabilize your spending and increase your borrowing power and find something that interests you. Invest in the business, stock, or product and gain financial success.

CHAPTER 13: Tips From a Wise Credit Repairman

Stop being a consumer. Commerce{ XE "Commerce" } is defined as the exchange of goods and services of value for a dollar. There are two sides to commerce.

1. The buyer's side, which is the consumer; and
2. The other is the seller.

Have you ever watched the classic movie Baby Boy staring Tyrese Gibson who played a pivotal role that defined the concept which was very true? Consumers take their money and stay in debt trying to keep up with the latest fad that doesn't even matter anymore once the consumer is done paying it off. Hip Hop Icon nas also quoted this in one of his rap songs when he spoke of corner hustlers, hustling to make purchases only to end up in prison and by the time they receive their freedom again. The purchase doesn't even matter because it's no longer a fad in the world. What a waste of time. A seller creates the product that the consumer purchases. In the movie *Wall Street*. These actors played an elusive role in how one consumer can turn an investment into a conglomerate. Oh yes it's cool to purchase your new

Miley Cyrus CD and a pair of Louboutins or Jordan Brand Air Jordan's or new Nike's but limit your wants until your investments are paying for your wants. The only difference in the rich and the poor is that the poor stays in debt and the rich invests their money into themselves or other businesses and most of the rich were once poor. Let your money work for you. Why do you think companies hand out surveys after your purchase of their products?

I'll tell you why. So they can find out what you like so they can create the product that will keep your account in the red while they enjoy financial freedom. Once a person likes a product they can convince another person to purchase the product. Word of mouth is the greatest promotion and consumers convince would be entrepreneurs into becoming consumers. Even if your just investing in your 401K. Most companies match your investment but you don't want to get into another scare like the crisis like the Enron scandal so you don't want to invest all of your money with your employer who might just be working for a greedy politician* Did you know that Dominoes Pizza was started with $7,500 in capitol and it failed to generate a profit during its first year. Did you know that Spike Lee financed his first film with $20,000 dollars from a credit card? Today he is worth hundreds of millions of dollars because of his willingness to establish and make timely payments which enabled him to persue his dreams by the use of credit.

Life can be demanding and it can be hard, but it can be a lot easier with the swipe of a credit card or a loan from the bank, or even the interest from a certificate of deposit. Although a lot could be done with a smartphone such as a Blackberry, a Galaxy, or an iPhone® 5. A lot more could be done with a 700 credit score. If you have any questions about the credit process, fill free to write me at the address in this book in the Acknowledgement section or visit me on face book.

Robert Boyd

CHAPTER 14: Freeing Up Capitol

The common law definition of capitol is known other than cold hard cash or assets or anything that can be used for value. Another reason which I have explained before for keeping good credit is to be able to free up much needed capitol. Imagine you're a corrections officer and your running low on funds. You're down to the last $40 dollars in daily activity funds and you hope the $40 lasts until your next paycheck. It's the middle of August and your ex wife is knocking on your door wanting money for school clothes for your son who starts school in a few days. A couple of days before your next paycheck. You've been enjoying life so much that you've forgotten that she needed $500 dollars for expenses such as backpacks, shoes, Levi jeans, pencils, ink pens, and other necessities needed for school. The normal idea to get out of the situation would be to either pawn a few objects or visit the local check advance for high interest rates but luckily for you. Last year you disputed your debts and now your credit score is around a 680 so your options aren't limited. You can either call the bank for a personal loan in which you can write her a check and get her away from your door step or drive to the ATM machine and draw out the borrowed money and you have saved the $40 dollars in capitol by using your credit. Let's give another example. You're a subpar millionaire and your LLC Company has a holding of $1.2 million in cash, $500,000 in assets, and a much expanded credit line. On a personal note, you have $200,000 in your 401K, $150,000 in your IRA, $200,000 in savings, and another $9,000 in your checking. Your company's expenses are around $60,000 per month and your profit is normally around $15,000 per month. You want to increase your revenue by adding a new line of machinery. Instead of putting cash up front, you decide to finance the equipment so that you can take the cash and hire exclusive maintenance personnel to aid you in making sure your company receives the best value out of its new machinery. You can also take the capitol that you saved to add to your human resource department and to add programs that help you find experienced workers that will help your company transition. With the extra profits from the new machinery, you can expand your business while paying on the principle of the new machinery and now your company is not headed for bankruptcy anytime soon. Skilled employees love to work for employers and executives who are able to make clear non- feeling decisions during hostile environments, because an employee is only as good as his employer and vice versa. Take Peyton Manning of the Denver Broncos for example who is undoubtedly one of the best quarterbacks of all time. True he can zip the ball at high speeds across the football canvas but no one ever talks about his linemen that do the blocking for him. Did you know that Peyton Manning has more pocket protection then any quarterback in the league which means that his line gives him more protection which equals more time to make clear decisions in who he wants to pass the ball to. Not to mention the receiver has to make the catch so even if Peyton throws the football right on target. There is no guarantee that the receiver will catch the ball. But by investing in top receivers, there is a greater chance that he will catch the ball. This is another example of why it is best to use your credit, so that you can take your capitol and do other things. Peyton Manning may be playing on a salary that was paid for by creditors while the linemen and the receivers are playing on cash that the company saved by using their credit to pay for Peyton's salary. 'Sounds a plan huh. With this concept the Colts went on to win a super bowl and the receiver nicknamed the glue enjoyed NFL success for years. It's the same in the work environment. A vast worker who can make keen decisions without being advised to do so. Even in everyday life. The Banks you choose and the credit cards you apply for as well as your employer and the people around you on a daily basis are your teammates believe it or not. Example, by making good choices you may save a lot of money, time, and embarrassment. Let's say you write a check that bounces because you lack the funds in your account to pay for the check and the bank charges you a fee for bounced checks of $50 dollars. Did you know that there are some banks that will cover the check and will not charge you a fee for up to 39 days? The fees and extra money was avoided because you chose a great bank or should I say a great teammate. So please read the fine print when applying for credit and remember. When it's time to save capitol, that doesn't mean you blow the extra money. No, the purpose is to invest the extra money in a business, a stock option, or something that will help you take the money and make it work for you.

A brokerage account to trade stocks can be opened free at www.TradeKings.com or through Wells Fargo Bank for a $25.00 fee. The cost of trading is one dollar per transaction whether you're trading one share or one million shares.

CHAPTER 15: Companies of Value That Require Minimal Investment

How many times have you ever driven by a Subway restaurant and thought, "Oh my I wish I had a million dollars to open one of those."

Did you know that with a 700 credit score, a $100,000 dollar credit line and about 50 to 70 thousand in cash, you are eligible to open your own Subway? The cash can be liquidated from your 401K or from refinancing your home.

Or what about a cleaning Franchise such as Jani King? Did you know that the minimum investment for a Jani King cleaning service is $10,000 in cash or a credit line of $15,000? That investment will help you make roughly $1,000 to $2,000 per month in guaranteed contracts secured by the franchise for you with annual fees at the end of the year. With the extra income, instead of purchasing that new Camaro and opting for the 3 to 5 year old one who's only difference is the dashboard and investing your monies or earned income into a franchise or company. Within a few years your money that you received from your tax refund that you invested into the Jani King will be making you thousands per month which will pay for your brand new Camaro. I like you, did not know this knowledge even though it's public record and available for you but now the dead has been awakened and it's time to do something about it.

To help you with deciding on which companies to choose from and their price range. I have listed a number of franchises that can be started with less than $100,000, cash and credit not withstanding McDonald's who's information I have provided as a bonus so that those with substantial income can have the knowledge to invest their massive fortunes into a franchise with wide economic growth. Here is the list of franchises and good luck on your way to financial freedom.

H & R block
Phone (816) 854-3000
Focus: Tax Preparation
Web: hrblock.com
Investment: $31,000 to $138,000

Jan Pro Franchising International
Phone: (678) 336-1780
Focus: Commercial Cleaning
Web: jan-pro.com
Investment: $3,000 to $50,000

Cruise One
Phone: (800) 892-3928
Focus: Travel Agency
Web: cruiseonefranchise.com
Investment: $4,000 to $50,000

Super Glass windshield Repair
Phone: (407) 240-1920
Focus: windshield repair
Web: Superglass.com
Investment: $10,000 to $35,000

McDonald's
Focus: Hamburgers and Fries
Phone: (630) 623-6196 Web: NA
Investment: $1 million to $2 million

Re/Max
Focus: Real Estate
Phone: (800) 525-7452
Web: remax.com
Investment: $35,000 to $200,000

Snap on Tools
Focus: Professional tools and equipment
Phone: (800) 786-6600
Web: snapon.com
Investment: $19,000 to $300,000

Chester's Chicken
Focus: Quick-Service Chicken Restaurant
Phone: (SCO) 646- 9403
Web: chestersintemational.com
Investment: $5,000 to $350,000

Fantastic Hair Salon
Focus: Full Service hair Salon
Phone: (877) 383-3831
Web: fantasticamsfranchise.com
Investment: $5,000 to $50,000

Chem-Dry Carpet and Upholstery Cleaning
Focus: Carpet, draping, and upholstery cleaning
Phone: (877) 307-8233
Web: Cemdry.com
Investment: $32,000 to $130,000

Mint Conditioning Franchising
Phone: (803) 548-6121

Focus: Janitorial Service
Web: mintcondition.com
Investment: $5,000 to $50,000

Cellairis Franchise
Phone: (678) 513-4020
Focus: Cell Phone repair
Web: cellairs.com
Investment: $35,000 to $200,000

Coffee News
Phone: (207) 941-0860
Focus: Coffee
Web: coffeenewsusa.com
Investment: $9,000 to $10,000

Complete Music
Phone: (300) 843-3366
Focus:
Web: cmusic.com
Investment: $10,000 to $50,000

7-Eleven
Phone: (800) 255-0711
Focus: Convenient store
Web: 7-eleven.com
Investment: $30,000 to $1.5 million

Subway
Focus: Sandwich and Salads
Phone: (800) 888-4848
Web: subway.com
Investment: $85,000 to $275,000

Computer Trouble Shooters
Phone: (877) 704 1702
Focus: small business technology
Web: comptroub.com

Investment; $17,000 to $75,000

Pizza Hut
Phone: (972) 338-8347
Focus: Pizza
Web: pizzahutfranchises.com
Investment: $295,000 to $1m

Mac Tools
Phone: (877) 622-8665
Focus: Automotive Tool Equipment
Web: mactool.com
Investment: $87,000 to $200,000

Express Professionals
Focus: Staffing
Phone: (877) 653-6400
Web: express franchising.com
Investment: $100,000 to $200,000

Senior Helpers
Focus: Personal homecare
Phone: (800) 760-6389
Web: seniorhelpers.com
Investment: $75,000 to $98,000

The Glass Guru
Focus: Window restoration and replacement
Phone: (916) 786-4878
Web: the glassguru.com
Investment: $27,000 to $118,000

Estrelli Insurance
Focus: Insurance
Phone: (888) 511-7722
Web; estrellainsurance.com
Investment: $50,000 to $85,000

Pilar to Post
Focus: Inspection Services
Web: pillartopost.com
Phone: (877) 963-2129
Investment: $10,000 to $50,000

Plan Ahead Events
Focus: Corporate event planning
Phone: (561) 868-1368
Web: discoverplanaheadadevents.com
Investment: $40,000 to $70,000

Realty Executives International
Focus: Real Estate
Phone: (800) 252-3366
Web: realtyexecutives.com
Investment: $20,000 to $120,000

Yellow Van Handy Man
Focus: Handyman fix it service
Phone: (206) 763-6800
Web: yellowvanhandyman.com
Investment: $19,000 to $35,000

Maid Brigade
Focus: Residential Cleaning
Phone: (800) 722-6243
Web: maidbrigade.com
Investment: $85,000 to $125,000

Tutor Doctor
Focus: Tutorial Services
Phone: (877) 988-8679
Web: tutordoctoropporunity. com
Investment: $67,000 to $170,000

Nestle Toll House Cafe
Focus: Cookies and Baked Goods

Phone:(214) 495-9533
Web: nestle.com
Investment: $150,000 to $415,000

AAmco Transmissions
Focus: Transmission Repair
Phone: (800)-292-8500
Web: aamco.com
Investment: $100,000 to $400,000

Baskin-Robbins
Focus: Ice Cream
Phone: (781) 737-3000
Web: baskinrobbins.com
Investment: $119,000 to $375,000

Papa John's
Focus: Pizza .
Phone: (502) 261-7272
Investment: $175,000 to $750,000

WSI Digital Marketing
Focus: internet Store
Phone: (888) 678-7588
Investment; $64,000 to $171,000

Knights Inn Hotel
Focus: Hotel
Phone: (973) 753-6000
Web: Knightsinn.com
Investment: $120,000 to $7m

Maaco Franchising
Focus: Automotive Paint Service
Phone: (800) 275-5200
Investment: $91,000 to '$500,000

Church's Chicken

Focus: Quick service chicken restaurant
Phone: (770) 350-3800
Investment: $191,000 to $1m

UPS/StoreMail Boxes ETC.
Focus: Postal business
Web: theups s tore. com
Phone: (858) 455-8800
Invesetment: $175,000 to $335,000

InXpress
Focus: Shopping Service
Web: inexpress.com
Phone: (801) 495-7894
Investment: $50,000 to $113,000

Certified Restoration Dry Cleaning Services
Focus: Textile-restoration services
Phone: (800) 520-2736
Investment: $45,000 to $240,000

Win Home Inspection
Focus:Home Inspection
Phone:(800) 967-8127
Investment: $42,000 to $67,000

Aire Master of America
Focus: Restroom deodorizing
Phone: (800) 525-0957
Web: airmaster.com
Investment: $35,000 to $130,000

Sports Image
Focus: Sports marketing for high schools
Phone: (937) 704-9670
Web: sportsimageinc.com
Investment: $15,000 to $40,000

Jet Black International
Focus: Asphalt Maintenance services
Phone: (888) 538-2525
Web: jet-black.com
Investment: $25,000 to $100,000

Tax Centers of America
Focus: Tax preparation
Phone: (479) 968-4796
Web: buylgetlfree.com
Investment: $20,000 to $65,000

Beuintal
Focus: Liquor inventing control service
Phone: (888) 238-4626
Web: beuintel.com
Investment: $37,000 to $55,000

Aanow Advertising
Focus: Advertising, sign spinning
Phone: (323) 944-2002
Web: (323) 944-2002
Investment: $37,000 to $80,000

Grout Doctor Global Franchise
Focus: Grout, tile, and stone care
Phone: (877) 476-8800
Web; groutdoctor.com
Investment: $16,000 to $40,000

Bookkeeping Express
Phone: (703) 766-5757
focus: Bookkeeping
Web: bookkeepingexpress.com
Investment: $40,000 to $60,000

Mainstream Boutique

Focus: Women's clothing
Phone: (952) 423-7344
Web: mainstreamboutique.com
Investment: $44,000 to $130,000

ERA Franchise Systems
Focus: Real Estate
Web: era.com
Phone: (973) 407-7904
Investment: $47,000 to $210,000

Oxifresh Franchising
Focus: Carpet cleaning
Phone: (877) 694-3737
Investment: $37,000 to $60,000

Assist 2 Sell
Focus: Real estate
Phone: (800) 528-7816
Web: assist2sell.com
Investment: $19,000 to $50,000

Midas International
Focus: Auto repair
Phone: (561) 383-3100
Web: midasfranchise.com
Investment: $85,000 to $390,000

These few companies will ensure you that your money will go to good use and not into fads that do nothing but increase your credit card debt. It is much better to live off of your profits of your own business than to live by working for your monies only to have your paycheck disappear because you don't know what to do with your money. When hiring employees. Hire employees that are driven such as yourself. Your employees are your teammates and in order for the company to grow. You will need employees who are willing to learn, listen, and take advantage of being a part of a winning team. Ford Motor company was able to avoid taking stimulus money during the auto world's near default of a downward economy left by the Bush Administration because of a joint effort of Human resource developers, CEO's, and employees who were all on the same accord. We witnessed the company grow and produce the best vehicles that money could buy without increasing their debt and Ford's stock price more than quad tripled because of this effect. I hope you have enjoyed a lesson that does not require a college degree although many attorneys learn the methods of filing disputes and winning civil claims in law school. There are even some attorney's that only practice Consumer litigation, so what you have learned in this book is a step by step analysis that most attorney's attend college for years to know. If you have any questions, I can be reached via mail at the address listed and I will respond to all inquires. Or log on to my Facebook page and don't be afraid to ask me a question about this process and I hope that you are on your way to financial freedom. The time is now, so what are you waiting for. The essence of a person is judged during their time of grief and not during their times of prosperity and a continued education is the only way to financial freedom. Don't forget to stay open-minded and base your thought process on common sense and not feelings. Trust your gut instinct and don't be afraid to ask questions. The dumbest question is the one that was never asked because Proper Preparation Prevents Poor Performance. I hope that you take the latter.

I'll see you in the top 41 percent of the world and I hope this knowledge that has never been revealed to the public, aids you in restoring your mental awareness as well as a road to financial freedom and some instant relief from being told "NO" whenever you try to make a move. Quitting and filing bankruptcy is not the option and when times get rough, that's when we as Americans get tougher. The time is now. Let's again review the step by step analysis.

1. Download or write the annual credit report{ XE "credit report" } services for a copy of your free credit report.

2. Fill out the application

3. Provide two proofs of I.D. and two verifications of your social security.

4. Open the report in the mail and file a dispute{ XE "dispute" } letter and send it certified mail to the lender, creditor, debt collector, or credit bureau.

5. Notify the credit bureau that the item or debt is in dispute{ XE "dispute" }.

6. After 60 days, send a cease and desist letter{ XE "dispute" } letter and then after 30 days, file a claim with the federal trade commission, (send copies and certified mail slips of dispute letters to the lender, debt collector, and credit bureau.

Please remember, that piggybacking is now considered illegal so disputing your credit and filing claims may be your only resource in obtaining the credit score you deserve. It's time for the middle class to stand up and take action. The time is now. I've made this book affordable to the average Joe or Jane, so that you are not left behind. The steps are here. What are you willing to do?

Remember, if a creditor, lender, or debt collector writes you a letter once you have disputed the debt or item and in the letter they don't provide you with a copy of the listed items pursuant to Title 15 Section 1666, or 15 U.S.C. 1692(g)(4). Mail them a dispute{ XE "dispute" } letter certified mail explaining to them that they have failed to validate the claim and send them a copy of the lawsuit for the violations that have occurred and title it notice of pending lawsuit. If they still do not comply, then your next step is to take civil action in Federal Court but this rarely happens. These companies do not want to spend their time litigating claims in court that they know they will lose but sometimes they are up for the fight but they can be taken down. God bless and good luck.

You may feel that you don't have time to do apply these standards but just remember that successful people have one thing in common. True, there is no blueprint towards being successful, but all successful people have a schedule.

They make time to do things of importance and those things of importance that only take minutes from their day. Sometimes, changes their whole lives. So be patient, President Obama wasn't elected President over night nor was Rome built overnight. Please be patient, open-minded, be willing, and most importantly, follow the schedule.

{NOTE: After you mail the dispute letter. Make sure you telephone (call) the creditor or debt collector to ensure that they have received your dispute letter. If the federal trade commission doesn't act promptly on your claim. Gather all your information (dispute letters, certified mail slips, etc. and mail them to:

CONSUMER FINANCIAL PROTECTION BUREAU
P.O.Box 4503
IOWA CITY, IA 52244

Make sure you send the copies and not original and they will process and handle your claim. After the process, visit the local IRS office and request a form 1099(a) cancelation of debt and tear off each of the invoices and mail them to the creditors and debt collectors. After this process, mail a letter to the IRS and us treasury with all copies requesting them in a letter titled LETER OF INSTRUCTION to zero out the accounts. (Must include all account numbers and addresses and name of creditors). You may also call the creditors and debt collectors to work out an agreement for a fraction of your debt to remove the debt item off your report for small monthly payments. Once you have cleared your negative items on your report. Draft a business plan and take it to the bank and if they like your idea. They will loan you the money for your business or to invest in a franchise. You may also seek help for your business through crowdfunding.com.

Remember the road to success is in your hands and is only 6 to 9 months away. Be innovative and take the ladder. I can be reached at Facebook at robertboydrobrun AND PLEASE SEARCH ME IN LOUISVILLE, KENTUCKY. The road to good credit starts today and remember if you have no credit. Follow my tips on how to build credit. Be motivated and when the drive gets tough. Then that's when we as innovators get tougher because giving up is not an option.

Robert Boyd

Application for Credit Consolidation Relief

(Money back guaranteed except for processing fee of 15 dollars)

I will reduce your debts by 85 percent guaranteed or you will be fully refunded. Send a $250 dollar money order to:

Robert Boyd
103 Marmak Drive
Glasgow, Kentucky 42141

or hit me up on Facebook.

Robert Boyd

Application for Credit Consolidation Relief

Name _____

Address _____

City _____

State _____ Zip _____

Phone _____

Debt Collector Name: _____

Debt Collector Address: _____

Owed Amount _____

Account Number: _____

Please send a copy of the student loan bill; it is required for prompt action. This is a service agreement between Robert Boyd and you to obtain debt relief.

Processing fees are $15.00 used for certified mailing. For a payment program, send $30.00 and we will bill you $30.00 per month for a total of 10 months.

Note: The credit dispute relief you are seeking will not be obtained until we have received your full $250 payment.

132

Application For Unathorized Inquiry Relief

(Money back guaranteed except for processing fee of $15)

"I will file your claims and will win the litigation by 100 percent guaranteed or you will be fully refunded. Send a $250 money order to:

Robert Boyd
103 Marmak Drive
Glasgow, Kentucky 42141

or hit me up on Facebook.

Robert Boyd

Application for Unauthorized Inquiry Relief

Name _____

Address _____

City _____

State _____ Zip _____

Phone _____

Company who posted Inquiry and their address

_____

_____

Date(s) Posted _____

Do you want to file a civil claim? _____ Yes _____ No

Please send me a copy of the credit report showing the unauthorized inquiry; it is required for prompt action. This is a service agreement between Robert Boyd and _____ to obtain unauthorized inquiry relief. Processing fees are $15.00 and we will bill you $30.00 per month for a total of 10 months.

Note: That the inquiry relief relief you request will not be obtained until we have received your full $250.00 payment.

INDEX

Robert Boyd

About the Author

Robert "Rob Run" Boyd known to many as Shawn Boyd and "KY" is a graduate of Caverna Independent High school. He attended college at Eastern Kentucky University and Draughons Junior College where he majored in Business management and Marketing and minored in Business Law. He is a member of the Feed The Children Foundation, Owens Chapel Baptist Church, owner of Most Hated Records, Publishing and Films, a song writer and a recording artist who has a soundtrack called *"Primo"* which can be downloaded for free on www.datpiff.com. He is

also an advocate for higher learning.

Most Hated Records, Publishing, and Films Presents:

A "KY" Production

HOW TO: Repair your credit in 180 days without filing bankruptcy or paying debt consolidators and win thousands of dollars in damages from, debt collectors and lenders who cannot legally obtain payment from you based on Title 15 U.S.C. § 1666 Of the United States Code and Title 15 U.S.C. 1692(e). What debt collectors and lenders of credit don't tell you and the secrets to stop them, even when you owe them. A step-by-step analysis revealed inside to re-establish your credit, quick and easy.

Your self-help guide to restoring your credit.

Learn how to reduce your student Loan and how to reduce your IRS tax lien after defaulting with your lender. All in this step-by-step guide to restoring your financial borrowing power.

Robert *"Rob Run"* Boyd

Robert Boyd

Coming Soon from Most Hated Records, Publishing, and Films

How to Repair Your Credit in 180 days (in stores now)

Primo: A hustlaz saga Primo II Primo III

Primo: The movie and soundtrack featuring Big V of the Nappy Roots

Deceitful Minds (Urban Christian)

Mimi and the Maserati Boyz

Bad Newz movie and soundtrack featuring
Mr. Serv of No Limit Records

My Sister's Boyfriend

It Girl

How to trade Stocks With Less Than $100 Dollars

Robert Boyd

To order *How to Repair Your Credit,*

Send $12.00 (free shipping and handling) to the address below:

Most Hated Records Publishing and Films
103 Marmak Drive
Glasgow, KY 42141

Or, order at Amazon.com

www.ingramcontent.com/pod-product-compliance
Lightning Source LLC
Chambersburg PA
CBHW070930210326
41520CB00021B/6878